Motivational Creative Writing

Building Skills with Imaginative Activities

by Athy Lionikis
and Lee Stevens

Incentive Publications, Inc.
Nashville, Tennessee

Illustrated by Gayle Harvey
Cover by John Schweikert
Edited by Patience Camplair

ISBN 978-0-86530-637-0

2   3   4   5   6   7   8   9   10   11   10   09   08

PRINTED IN THE UNITED STATES OF AMERICA
www.incentivepublications.com

Table of Contents

Introduction 7

Activities to Get You Started 11
    The Hat Trick 12
    The Comic Book 17

More Activities 23
    Magic 4-Square 24
    Postcard Journey 27
    Stained Glass Mosaic 30
    Put a Lid on It! 33
    Dialogue 36
    Alter Ego 39
    Cubes 41
    123–321 Switch 49
    Dance Line 51
    Cuneiform 54
    Cyclone Stories 59
    Greek Vases 63
    Last Straw! 66
    The Pirate Ship Battle 70
    Treasure Map 73
    Entangled in the Web 76
    Freedom is a Gift 79
    Groucho 82
    Ibis of Peace 85
    Group of 3 90
    Patriotic American Flag 92
    Star Ship Shuttle 97

Methods **105**

What Good Creative Writing Looks Like 106

Things to Remember When Setting the Mood for Your Story 109

Brainstorming Worksheet 110

The Critics' Corner 111

From Brainstorm to Story Line 112

Story Line—Parts One and Two 113

The Construction Zone 115

Modeling by Talking and Thinking Aloud 116

The Memory Game 117

Graphic Organizers and Brainstorming 118

The Spider Web 119

Made-Up Creative Words 120

Creative Lettering 121

"It's the Plumber" 122

Plumb a Phone: An Editing Tool 124

Publishing **127**

Accordion Books 128

To Make a Book 130

Package Deal 133

On the Ball 138

Picture Frame 142

The Box 143

Starburst 145

Tips for Art and the Finished Product 151

Rubrics **153**

About Rubrics 154

Creative Writing Rubric 155

Best Rubric Yet! 156

Sample Writing Rubric 157

Oral Presentation Rubric 158

Rubric Form and Scoring Guide 159

INTRODUCTION

How to Use this Book

Motivational Creative Writing is designed to encourage student interest in literature and writing while increasing their knowledge and success in using the writing process. These high-energy activities and creative finished products will capture the attention of your students, making learning (and teaching) enjoyable and rewarding.

This book's unique approach to creative writing incorporates a wide variety of activities that all build on the basics of the writing process. Each activity includes a statement of purpose and ideas for introducing the assignment, along with applicable cross-curricular uses and "twists and turns"—variations that will open up new possibilities and add excitement to the project. The step-by-step directions will guide you as you lead your class in each activity.

The "Methods" we have selected will support you in teaching writing skills. These pages are filled with practical tips and tools to help your students build a solid foundation in the writing process, from organizing their thoughts and choosing the most vivid descriptors, to editing their own work as well as that of others.

In the "Publishing" section, you will find a number of designs for a finished writing project. Allow your students to use their imaginations when choosing a format. Although suggestions for the finished products are included for each activity, these publication techniques are easily adaptable and can be used with almost any creative writing project and across the curriculum.

The final section of the book includes some approaches to assessment. The "Rubrics" section presents samples, ideas for building original rubrics, and even guidelines for incorporating the Creative Writing Standards into your evaluations of students' work.

A new world of *Motivational Creative Writing* awaits you and your students. We hope you will find it as useful and enjoyable as we have!

Capturing the Imagination with Creative Writing

Comics, animation, and fantasy have had an amazing run of popularity over the last 60 years. Their heroes have become household names, and so has some of the creative language they have introduced. We are all familiar with the sound of the "Road Runner" or the theme from "Popeye." Odds are that your students can name more characters in the "Peanuts" comic strip than you can characters in any Jack London novel!

Kids (young and old) want to be entertained at every turn of their life. Young minds are titillated, stimulated, mesmerized, hypnotized, and homogenized by an industry that has capitalized on the fantastic in order to keep their interest. Many times, capturing the attention of a young creative person puts the teacher in the position of being the learner. Teachers must keep up-to-date on modern language usage and key in to students' interests in order to motivate them in the creative writing process.

Our motivational creative writing curriculum capitalizes on students' imaginations, energy, and inclination toward the world of comics, animation, and fantasy. This book is filled with the activities, methods, and production techniques that will bring success and satisfaction to your students while training them in the writing process.

Many studies have been conducted on the topic of brain function and thinking modalities. We have found that the "right-brain" style of teaching, with a heavy dose of the random/abstract proves to be the most effective and productive approach to creative writing. When students write from the freedom of the random/abstract, they lose their inhibitions. Everyone can be successful in our motivational, interactive, and fun approach to creative writing as "failures" and "mistakes" are accepted, eliminated, disguised, and redirected. Students' peers become their teachers and critics, and as they learn from one another, each can celebrate in the ownership of a quality finished product.

Recent research has proven the importance of movement and abstract thought for achieving a higher order of thinking. The accuracy of this theory is reinforced by observing the increase of energy and focus of middle grades students when these two techniques are incorporated into the writing curriculum. The more creative arts are plugged into the students' writing experience, the more comfortable their focus becomes, and the quality of product improves.

Thus, our motivational creative writing curriculum relies on a lot of hands-on art. Incorporating art, theater, and creative writing only releases more of the "creative juices" that help students visualize themes and characters in their writing. If the visualization of art and the movement of theater do not come into play in a creative writing exercise, students cannot reach their full creative potential. Each individual has unique talents, and therefore some students will be more artistic or more theatrical than others. Create a cadre of student helpers who have mastered a certain art or theater technique, and send them out as "Ambassadors of Learning" in order to help other students through peer teaching. Student-to-student teaching and learning is also a crucial part of the cooperative learning model.

Creating a story is often a group or cooperative learning endeavor. The activities in this resource lend themselves to group efforts. The writer, the editor and the artist can collaborate to produce a shared project. Students (or the whole class) can meet together to brainstorm ideas, produce an outline, and edit the story. The artwork will follow along with the story line (rough draft), and the sketches, dialogue and word balloons are set in place. The final step is to "publish" a unique finished format, complete with the final art and the edited copy.

All components of the six-step writing process are hidden in the fun of the production, and this approach has met with great success for all students. In addition, we have designed these motivational creative writing techniques with national standards in mind. Each activity has been planned with a purpose and cross-curricular themes incorporated throughout, which can be easily matched to the creative writing standards.

As you employ the standards in conjunction with these lively and diverse activities, students' creative writing skills will grow along with their imaginations. The result will be quality writing and attractive finished products that will be a source of pride for you and your students.

ACTIVITIES TO
GET YOU STARTED

◆————————————————————————◆

- The Hat Trick
- The Comic Book

"The Hat Trick" and "The Comic Book"
are this program's signature presentations!

The Hat Trick

This creative writing activity is popular with students and teachers alike. The lesson is high-interest and always successful when followed through with one of the formats provided in the "Publishing" section of this book. The teacher and class will need to do quite a bit of fun prepwork. When assembling a collection of hats, remember: the more bizarre the hat, the more students will engage in the creative atmosphere.

PURPOSE:

- To promote cooperative learning
- To carry through to a finished publication
- To encourage writing through the use of fantasy
- To promote creativity
- To encourage the thought process through brainstorming
- To use the visualization process
- To practice storytelling and clarity
- To learn the writing processes with the help of peer editing

CROSS-CURRICULAR USES:

- Language classes and the use of dialogue
- Social studies: place characters in a historical setting
- Art: sketch portraits of the student wearing hats
- Student Council promotions.

MATERIALS:

- A collection of hats
  (Ask fellow teachers, students, and friends to donate unusual hats from their closets or attic.)

- 3" x 5" index cards and yarn
- Markers or felt-tip pens
- Materials for final publication
  (see pages 127–151)

12

You can use any hat—from a football helmet to a court jester's cap. Once you have a good assortment of hats, have the class choose one and brainstorm a name for a character who would wear such a hat. At this time, it is important to brainstorm a short sentence describing the who, what, and where of the character (for example, "Helga the Horrible" Queen of the Amazon Vixons).

STEP·BY·STEP

1. Write the agreed upon name and descriptive sentence on one side of a 3" x 5" index card, and a number on the other.

2. Hole punch one end of the 3" x 5" index card and tie a piece of yarn through the hole.

3. Attach each name card to the appropriate hat.

4. Place or hang the hats around the room in a decorative manner.

5. Make the number of cards that matches the number of hats you have, and drop them into one of your hats.

6. Have students draw a number, find the appropriate hat, and return to their desks, wearing their hats.

7. One at a time, each student will rise (wearing his or her hat) and introduce themselves, assuming the persona of the character whose name has been placed on the index card.

8. After the introductions, students return the number that they pulled from the hat.

9. Randomly pull three numbers at a time from the hat, and those wearing the matching numbered hat become partners in creating a story that includes each of their characters.

10. The first of the three becomes the hero of the story, the second is the villain, and the third plays the person in distress.

Motivational Creative Writing

The Hat Trick

11. Send the groups of three to different areas of the room to brainstorm a plot using their characters. Make it clear that this is a cooperative learning lesson and the students must adhere to the classroom guidelines for this type of learning.

12. Once the plot has been decided, character development is the next step. Use the worksheet included on the following page.

13. Each member of the group contributes to all characters, plot, and setting.

14. The story usually self-starts at this point and can be given as a cooperative learning lesson and group project, or assigned individually. (The individual assignment lends itself to more publication choices.)

15. Students return to their desks to start their rough drafts.

16. When the students complete their rough draft, they are ready for their first rewrite.

17. Move to the "Critics' Corner." Refer to the outline provided on page 16.

18. Once all story lines have been shared, students should return to their desks and make the corrections that have been offered by their peers in the "Critics' Corner."

19. Now it is time for the groups of three to put on a "mini-play" of their story. This is easily done if the writing is a cooperative project, but quick "read-overs" of individual stories and a little more prep time is all that is needed to address individual stories. It is important to set up a few ground rules and not let too much acting take place (80% dialogue and 20% acting is a good rule of thumb). Students tend to get really active, with fight scenes or inappropriate dialogue.

20. Now it is time to choose the right publishing format in which to write the final drafts. All publishing activities will require another editing step (the "Construction Zone," page 121). Look in the "Publishing" section (pages 127–151) for some good ideas, or incorporate this lesson with the "Comic Book" activity beginning on page 17.

TWISTS AND TURNS

- "The Hat Trick" is really fun when produced as a play! Students should complete the written piece in the form of a script. This is a great way to teach dialogue.

- You can use the hat collection to lighten up the faculty meetings or for an impromptu costume party.

- Wear a different hat each day to greet your class, and have students write a quick response about how they felt when they saw you.

- This activity is a great to be used as an "icebreaker."

Character Development

Remember to describe the hat, clothing, body language, speech, setting, scenery, and any unusual traits belonging to each character!

CHARACTER #1

  IMPRESSIONS:

  DIALOGUE:

CHARACTER #2

  IMPRESSIONS:

  DIALOGUE:

CHARACTER #3

  IMPRESSIONS:

  DIALOGUE:

Motivational Creative Writing

Critics' Corner

The "Critics' Corner" is an effective way for students to share their prewriting with peers and come away with some positive ideas about improving their final copy. "The Hat Trick" can be authored by a group or by individuals taking each character in a direction of their choosing. Adjust the "Critics' Corner" to your own lesson plan. The rules are simple and effective.

STEP·BY·STEP

1. Students will meet as groups of three. Give students plenty of room to spread out—in a corner of the room or in the hallway, etc. Students may sit "knees together" (in a circle) to help them concentrate and stay focused.

2. Each group will elect a member to serve as the "anchor." This student will be in charge of the group and keep the members on task.

3. Next, each student will read his or her story aloud to the group. The reader will stop and answer questions about anything that is unclear or that the listeners do not understand. At this time, each member of the group will also have the chance to give some positive input.

4. In their small group, each student is required to take note of the questions and make a record of the parts of the story that are not clear to the listeners.

5. This process is repeated until all story lines have been shared and any corrections and additions have been noted.

6. Each "sharing" will end with at least three positive statements from the listeners before the next sharing begins.

7. When all sharing has been completed, the members will return to their seats and make the improvements to their own story lines.

The Comic Book

Comics have had an amazing run in popularity for the last 60 years! Comic book heroes have become household names, and so has some of the creative language that they have introduced. This writing activity incorporates the 5- to 7-step writing process into a comic book format.

PURPOSE:

- To promote cooperative learning
- Language arts skills such as editing, punctuation, sequencing, sentence structure, grammar, spelling, and dialogue
- To encourage creativity and teach basic art skills
- To inspire clarity
- To show the pride of ownership in a finished published product
- Compacting
- Advancing interdisciplinary skills

CROSS-CURRICULAR USES:

- Dialogue in English, foreign languages, and ESL classes
- Social studies reports and projects
- Science research papers
- Exploratory classes
- Reports in any subject
- Problem solving across the curriculum

MATERIALS:

- Colored pencils
- #2 pencils
- Fine-tip black marking pens
- Soft gum erasers
- Scissors
- Glue sticks
- Lined notebook paper
- Large sheets of blank newsprint paper
- Large white paper (flip chart size)
- Laminating film

17

The Comic Book

1. Brainstorm a topic. Direct the class to write down as many ideas as they can in a 5-minute period. Use the "Brainstorming Worksheet" found on page 110. Remember, no idea is a bad idea. Have a volunteer write the ideas on the blackboard or a flip chart. Do not worry about spelling during the brainstorming session.

2. Once the topic is established, go to the "Brainstorming Worksheet" and continue brainstorming—heroes, villains (and their superpowers), characters, settings, etc., following the worksheet guides. Take a look at the "Viking Character Ideas" (page 20) as an example.

3. Students can now select their setting, characters, and powers using the list they generated to begin the rough draft of their stories.

4. At this time you can introduce creative language using the format indicated on the "Made-Up Creative Words" instruction sheet on page 120.

5. Once students have a rough draft of their story, it is time for editing using the "Critics' Corner" technique.

6. After students have met in the "Critics' Corner," they should go back to their seats and make the suggested corrections.

7. It is now time to transfer stories onto large newsprint paper using the "Story Line" forms found on pages 113–114. This method is used by moviemakers, cartoonists, and authors to arrange the order of their writing for clarity. It helps students separate their story into the beginning, middle, and end; arrange their copy; and sketch in their art work. Remind students to work big when they do their illustrations. There should be a picture on each page to illustrate that part of the story.

8. The teacher proofs the story line and makes any suggestions necessary for clarity and grammar that may have been missed.

9. When it is time to publish the final draft, remind students:
   a. Sketch lightly in pencil so that mistakes can be easily erased.
   b. Type the story and cut it to fit on each page of the chosen publication form.
   c. Set and lightly mark where the text will go, but do not glue it down yet.
   d. Draw large illustrations; students always tend to want to work small. Remind them that they do not need to be great artists—even stick people work nicely. Visit "Tips for Art and the Finished Product" (page 151).

Motivational Creative Writing

e. When it is time to color, remember to use colored pencils (not markers). Outlining the drawing with a black fine-tip marker will give it a more finished look. The key is neatness, working large, coloring heavily, and outlining in black.

f. Now books are ready to be folded and reviewed. Students should look over their books and exchange them with other students for a final edit in the "Construction Zone" (page 115), making any changes that are suggested.

g. Put laminating film over the cover, and the product is complete!

TWISTS AND TURNS

- Adopt one superhero to represent the class
- Hold mock elections, one class's superhero vs. another class's
- Invent mottoes and slogans for the superhero
- Make an ongoing comic strip, weekly or monthly
- Superhero dress-up day
- Produce a "funny paper" for the school newspaper
- Make superhero logos, a superhero costume, and a mascot
- Superhero inventive language, sayings, or words (SHAZAAM!)
- Superhero "baseball cards" (for collecting, trading, or gaming)
- Superhero "website" linking other superhero sites
- Computer presentations
- Superhero "greeting," secret handshake, codes
- Superhero play
- Comic book day—bring in as many as you can, share the class's too
- Authors can share their comic books with children in the lower grades

Now, your ideas!

_____

_____

_____

_____

_____

_____

Motivational Creative Writing

Viking Character Ideas

- Sky King the Viking
- Psych King the Viking
- Ike the Vike
- Ski King the Viking
- The Hurricane Dane
- Steed the Swede
- The Insane Dane
- The Chrome Dome from Stockholm
- Dane the Brain
- I Got Game, Dane
- The Great Dane
- The Incredible Sven
- Heide the Horrible
- My Way or Norway
- Walmart or Denmark
- Scandal-Navia
- Iceman from Iceland
- The Helsinki Pinky
- Slinky of Helsinki

Story Titles and Ideas

- Bored on the Fjord!
- The Great Dane, (And I do not Mean the Dog!)
- The Adventures of Sky King the Viking vs. Big Hand Hans!
- Hurricane Dane, Another Big Blow!
- Yes, the Dane has Got Game!
- Dane the Brain—Not just Another Pretty Face!
- Chrome Dome from Stockholm Meets Ike the Vike!

Character Drawing Ideas

For the student who is stuck, or thinks he or she cannot draw, on the next page are some ideas to use. Just blow them up, and allow each student to personalize his or her own characters by making some changes to the drawings and coloring them.

Motivational Creative Writing

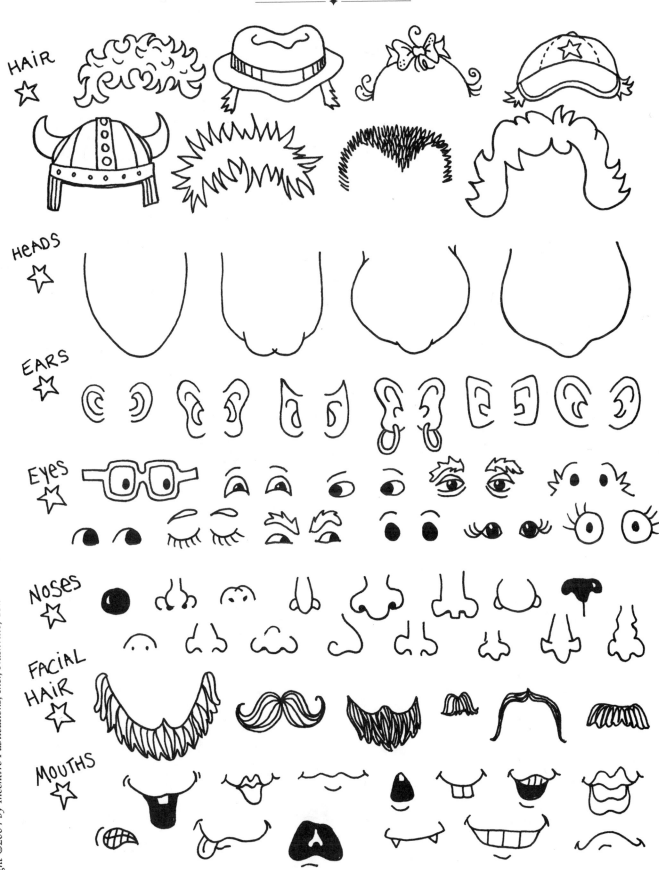

HAIR ☆

HEADS ☆

EARS ☆

EYES ☆

NOSES ☆

FACIAL HAIR ☆

MOUTHS ☆

Motivational Creative Writing

MORE ACTIVITIES

- Magic 4-Square
- Postcard Journey
- Stained Glass Mosaic
- Put a Lid on It!
- Dialogue
- Alter Ego
- Cubes
- 123–321 Switch
- Dance Line
- Cuneiform
- Cyclone Stories
- Greek Vases
- Last Straw
- The Pirate Ship Battle
- Treasure Map
- Entangled in the Web
- Freedom is a Gift
- Groucho
- Ibis of Peace
- Group of Three
- Patriotic American Flag
- Star Ship Shuttle

Magic 4-Square

The concept behind the "Magic 4-Square" is for the student to be able to read or write a short story and condense it into a 4-square picture story. The object is to record the beginning, a 2-part middle, and the ending to the story, including the parts most important to the theme. Creating this "story line" is vital for the student to visualize and express their comprehension of the written piece. Students then make up questions about the story using the 4-square pictures as the guide for their answers. Once a student learns to visualize a story and verbalize it in his or her own words, comprehension levels will soar! Not only this—they will have assumed ownership of the product!

PURPOSE:

There are many great uses for this seemingly simple lesson. This can be a powerful presentation when a high-interest lesson is needed. Here is a list of ideas, and you can brainstorm many more.

- Class starters
- Observations
- Comprehension
- Compaction
- Key points

- Problem solving
- Social studies
- 4-part flash cards
- Character education

- Dialogue
- Foreign language
- Scientific thinking
- ESL
- Comic story

CROSS-CURRICULAR USES:

Use this activity in all curricular areas.

MATERIALS:

- White computer paper
- Colored pencils

- Black fine-tip markers
- Laminating paper

- Scissors

There are several ways to present this activity. Adapt the beginning to your group.

STEP·BY·STEP

1. Brainstorm the topic for a creative writing short story, and have students write to fit the topic. Or, select short stories and have the students read and condense the story using their own words. Before long, teachers have a file full of short stories that can be used for this step. Using another author's story relieves the pressure of having to write one's own story, and speeds up the project completion process.

2. Once the story is rewritten in the student's own words, it can be considered the rough draft and must be edited for clarity and correctness. "Critics' Corner" or "Construction Zone" editing may be used for this step. (See pages 111, 115.)

3. Once the final draft of the condensed story is agreed upon, students rewrite or type it into a final copy.

4. Fold a piece of copy paper so the paper is divided into one ¾ section and one ¼ section. Fold the ¼ section back so that all that is showing is the larger piece. Divide this section into 4 equal windows, as if it is a 4-part comic strip. See example on page 26.

5. Students draw their "mind's eye" representation of the story, including the important characters, setting, theme, and some dialogue.

6. Color the drawings and outline in sharp-tipped marking pen as described in "Tips for Art and the Finished Product" (page 151).

7. Students brainstorm 5 to 7 comprehension questions that can be asked about the 4-Square picture story. This part allows for creativity—ask the reader to predict what the story is about according to the pictures on the 4-Square.

8. The questions from step 7 are written on the ¼ flap of the paper and when folded back, the questions will be on the reverse side of the drawings, and students will need to exercise recall in order to answer the questions.

9. Laminate the projects and collect them where they can be studied and enjoyed by students in their free time.

Motivational Creative Writing

Magic Four Squares

TWISTS AND TURNS

- Use this activity to tell a creative writing story, or to tell the life story of a famous person or the events leading up to an important historical happening.

- Demonstrate directions in four stages or show the steps in a problem-solving strategy.

- This activity is a great "starter" and can be used several times throughout the year.

Motivational Creative Writing

Postcard Journey

The fold-down postcard technique teaches students how to summarize and "key in" on main ideas or important facts. It incorporates art, manual dexterity, symmetry, and problem solving, and is a great activity for reports on historical places, events in history and science, or reports on famous people. This technique is a super project to review key facts of a field trip or a social studies lesson. The presentation can be folded shut, addressed, stamped, and mailed through the U.S. Postal Service. Grandparents would enjoy receiving a well-done travelog as an example of their student's schoolwork.

PURPOSE:

- To teach summarizing and condensing of facts
- To identify key facts
- To showcase a travelog
- To focus on clarity
- To promote problem solving

CROSS-CURRICULAR USES:

This activity can be used in all core and exploratory classes as:

- Mini-research reports
- Book reports
- Video notes
- Movie reviews
- Creative writing short stories
- Math concepts
- Picture diaries

Address and mail the postcards for a letter writing activity!

MATERIALS:

- A large piece of white flip chart paper (24" x 36")
- Colored pencils
- Black fine-tip markers

Postcard Journey

Fold a sheet of white flip chart paper (24" x 36") into thirds lengthwise. Cut along the folds to form three long strips. Fold each strip into eight sections, accordion-style. One sheet of paper makes three books of eight sections each. The first section is to be used for the cover and the next seven are for the mini-reports and their art.

☆ Use 24" x 36" flip chart paper.

☆ Fold it into thirds lengthwise.

☆ Cut on folds into 3 long strips.

☆ Fold each strip into 8 sections.

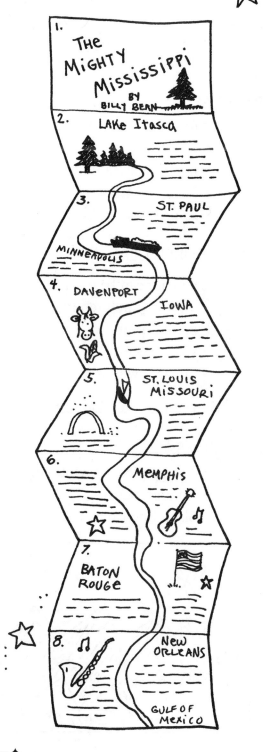

1. THE MIGHTY Mississippi BY BILLY BERN
2. LAKE ITASCA
3. ST. PAUL
   MINNEAPOLIS
4. DAVENPORT
   IOWA
5. ST. LOUIS MISSOURI
6. MEMPHIS
7. BATON ROUGE
8. NEW ORLEANS
   GULF OF MEXICO

1. Choose any seven terms, places, events, or people from the list brainstormed by the class or the list given by the teacher.

2. Complete a short research investigation into each topic.

STEP·BY·STEP

3. Condense the information into one or two short paragraphs. Write a rough draft and take it to the "Critics' Corner."

4. Type and save the edited written report.

5. Place the cutout paragraph on the postcard and outline its position in pencil. Before gluing the report, students must share their work in the "Construction Zone" and make any final changes.

6. Sketch (in pencil) the artwork that represents each mini-report.

7. When all drawings and information is positioned, color drawings darkly with colored pencils.

8. Trace the outline of the drawings with a fine-tip marker. See "Tips for Art and the Finished Product" (page 151) for more help in making a great-looking final product.

9. You can decorate the reverse side or use the reports as real postcards—write a message and mail them.

TWISTS AND TURNS

- Scientific processes and formulas

- Life stories of famous scientists

- A postcard journey exploring different animal and plant life

- Algebraic terms and geometrical theories

- A road trip diary during field trips or any study trip

- Design a single postcard with a drawing on the front and a message about the drawing on the back. The message should include six facts about the subject, then be addressed and mailed. If it is an assignment that is for the grade book, have the students mail it to you in care of the school.

Motivational Creative Writing

Stained Glass Mosaic

This can be used as a motivational starting place for students writing a creative story or a report. The mosaic is also a great way to display an original poem or a one-page story.

PURPOSE:

- To stimulate students' interest in a subject
- To showcase students' work
- To provide a springboard for creative writing

- To stimulate research
- To promote mental imagery
- To use as a prompt in foreign language study
- To teach sequencing

CROSS-CURRICULAR USES:

This activity can be used in all core and exploratory classes as:

- Research project starters
- Reports on people, places, or things (for example, the Statue of Liberty, presidents, a famous artist, Martin Luther King, Taj Mahal, Pyramids of Giza, Rock of Gibraltar, animals, planets, rocks, maps)
- Book reports
- Creative writing story ideas

- Descriptive writing
- Speech starters for a public speaking presentation
- Writing biographies
- Foreign language description
- Social studies/art "stained glass windows"

MATERIALS:

- Scissors
- Glue stick
- Black construction paper

- Additional various colors of construction paper
- Pictures cut from magazines, postcards or original art
- Laminating machine or laminating sheets

This is a wonderful motivational activity for students and can be approached in several ways. One way is to brainstorm a topic and subject and imagine the most important scene or character. Teach this mental imaging by using the "Modeling by Talking and Thinking Aloud" method with the class (see page 116).

Another way is to use pictures from magazines, postcards, or students' art as a springboard for researching a report, writing a descriptive paragraph, learning to write biographies, choosing topics for a speech, or describing a picture in a foreign language.

Students use their pictures and write their stories or reports. Remember to use the rough draft, "Critics' Corner," and "Construction Zone" formats (pages 111 and 115).

When the writing component is completed, the students are to use the following steps to create their stained glass mosaic.

☆ Sketch your picture in pencil.

☆ Color with colored pencils...

☆ ...and outline in marker.

STEP·BY·STEP

1. Using regular copy paper, lightly sketch the chosen scene or character (or use pictures from magazines or postcards).

2. When drawing, use pencil, sketch lightly, and fill the whole page.

3. Color the drawing with colored pencils, not markers. Remember to color heavily.

4. Outline in fine-tip black marking pen.

5. When the drawing is finished, turn the paper over. Using a pencil and ruler, draw a grid on the back side of about 1″ to 1½″ squares.

☆ Turn your picture over...

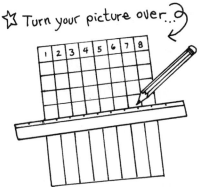

☆ ...and draw a grid on the back.

Stained Glass Mosaic

6. Number the squares 1, 2, 3, etc., beginning in the top left corner, until all are systematically numbered.

7. Cut the squares out until the entire drawing has been cut into 1" squares.

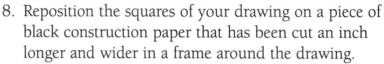

☆ Cut apart the squares.

8. Reposition the squares of your drawing on a piece of black construction paper that has been cut an inch longer and wider in a frame around the drawing.

☆ Then glue them in order on your paper.

9. Carefully glue the cut-apart picture back together, leaving a small pane of black showing between each square.

10. The result should resemble a leaded glass window.

TWISTS AND TURNS

• Cut the mounted pictures into shapes or squares and put the pieces into envelopes to use as a sequencing problem-solving activity. This can be used as a springboard to promote brainstorming for the writing piece.

• Cut up Christmas cards and reposition them as mosaics mounted on green or red construction paper. Have the students write a Christmas message or poem and mount it to the back of the mosaic.

• This is an excellent social studies activity when studying the construction of great cathedrals and the use of stained glass.

Motivational Creative Writing

Put a Lid on It!

"Put a Lid on It!" stimulates the creative juices that need to flow in order to brainstorm the many directions that this project can take. The lesson involves following directions carefully—listening, viewing, and reading. Once students learn how to fold the box, teachers will have a hard time slowing their creativity and interest in the artistic part of this writing lesson.

The story that is written and hidden in the box can take on many forms. The story line can be well-suited for dialogue, pros and cons, study questions and answers, and many other applications.

PURPOSE:
- To develop problem-solving skills by following directions, which includes visual, listening, and writing skills
- To use origami to construct the box
- To brainstorm the subject matter and its presentation
- To promote clarity and fluency

CROSS-CURRICULAR USES:
- Language arts: stories, poems
- Book reports or a report in any subject area
- Math and science: to demonstrate volume, solid and plane geometry
- Art
- Debates
- Dialogue
- Foreign language
- Social studies: to compare and contrast; examine religions, famous persons, geography, and cultures; to construct timelines

Put a Lid on It!

MATERIALS:

- Paper of any kind and size (Colored construction paper is good, but the heavy gauge is difficult to bend and crease sharply. Magazine pages work well!)
- Scissors
- Markers, pencil, crayons, black marker for outlining
- Feathers, glitter, ribbon, or any other kind of decorations

1. With students, brainstorm some ideas that will tie in with the focus of your lesson.

STEP-BY-STEP

2. Students select their topic and complete a rough draft.

3. Take the rough draft to "Critics' Corner."

4. Revisit the areas addressed in "Critics' Corner."

5. Fold the base of the box as described in "The Box" (see page 143).

6. Type the edited piece of writing, with the margins set so the column of the text will fit inside the box.

7. Cut a strip of paper slightly smaller than the inside of base of the box.

8. Determine how long the strip needs to be so that your report or story will fit. (Leave room for illustrations.)

9. Fold the strip of paper accordion-style so that the entire strip will fold neatly into the box.

10. Mount the paragraphs of the story and pictures on the face of each fold.

11. The last revision takes place in the "Construction Zone."

12. Make all your final changes before gluing it onto the inside of the box top and bottom. (Corrections can always be retyped, cut, and pasted.)

13. Make a lid using the directions for "The Box."

14. Decorate the outside of the box.

15. Display and share with the class.

TWISTS AND TURNS

- Build boxes of different sizes, one inside the other, each including either the beginning, middle, or end of the story.

- Include a secret message inside the box that can be found through clues in the story.

- Decorate the box like a pirate's treasure chest to hold the creative writing story.

- In math and science, the maker of the box can put an object inside it and choose a partner who guesses what is inside. Clues can be found in the decorations and theme of the box, and by its weight, sound, and smell. Allow the person guessing to ask three yes or no questions. Each question asked results in a loss of points.

- Put a comic strip inside.

Dialogue

This activity engages students' creativity while focusing on keeping the dialogue flowing with the ideas encouraged by their half of a drawing or portrait.
This is a simple, powerful, and fun way to teach dialogue that will keep the students focused and involved.

PURPOSE:

- To develop skills for writing dialogue in the correct manner
- To examine two sides of a conversation as it develops
- To incorporate problem solving into the dialogue process
- To combine the use of insight with the writing scheme
- To create and develop unique characters and conversations

CROSS-CURRICULAR USES:

- Language arts: creative writing, autobiographies
- Art: portrait or character drawing
- Advisory activity: character education
- Science, social studies, music, and physical education: autobiographies
- Computer technology: word processing and formatting
- Foreign language: dialogue and vocabulary drills

MATERIALS:

- Scissors
- White construction paper
- Sketching pencils and colored pencils
- Black fine-tip pen
- Colored construction paper
- Glue

Motivational Creative Writing

1. Students fold a piece of copy machine paper in half the "hot dog" way.

2. Students draw and color two characters, one on either side of the fold. In order to be consistent, the characters must be drawn the length of the student's hand, from fingertip to the heel of their palm. Each character will be centered to fit on one half of the folded piece of paper.

3. The finished drawing stands on its V-fold with a different character facing each of a pair of students who are sitting opposite one another at a desk. Students adopt the personality of the character facing them.

4. Their character's expression and appearance might depict a specific emotion; the conversationalists can expand on this to create a whole personality.

5. The two students develop and write a conversation between their characters by passing a piece of notebook paper back and forth, keeping in mind the personality and possible responses of the character they have adopted.

6. Skipping lines should naturally occur within the written dialogues, which subtly demonstrates the correct paragraphing of dialogue.

7. A few directions about quotation marks, commas, periods, and mentioning who is speaking at each paragraph will encourage well-written dialogue.

Motivational Creative Writing

8. Type the completed dialogue and mount it on a piece of construction paper on the reverse side of the character drawing.

9. Do not forget to run the written piece through the "Critics' Corner" for peer editing.

10. The "Plumb a Phone" (pages 124–125) is a great self-editing tool to use before final production.

TWISTS AND TURNS

• The momentum of this dialogue can guide the writer into a creative writing story.

• Students can also have a neighbor draw them or use self-portraits as the basis for the conversation.

• Photos of famous people can be cut and pasted onto the folded copy machine paper, with the conversations developed in the same manner.

Alter Ego

In this activity, students let their creativity flow into supplying ideas encouraged by the possibilities presented by the missing half of a portrait. Imagining that one half of the face depicts the subject's normal demeanor and the other half depicts their "alter ego," students generate an alternative personality and appearance for their portrait. When the creative writer draws the missing half and creates a story to go along with the two personalities, fantastic results will follow.

PURPOSE:
- To develop a character with more than one personality, and to write a creative story using both of the egos
- To promote a writing activity that includes two versions of a single story
- To incorporate problem solving into the brainstorming process
- To use insight into the writing process
- To create unique characters

CROSS-CURRICULAR USES:
- Language arts: creative writing, autobiographies
- Art: portrait or character drawing
- Advisory activity: character education
- Science, social studies, music, and physical education: biographies
- Computer technology: word processing and formatting

MATERIALS:
- Pictures of faces from magazines
- Scissors
- White construction paper
- Sketching pencils or colored pencils
- Glue sticks

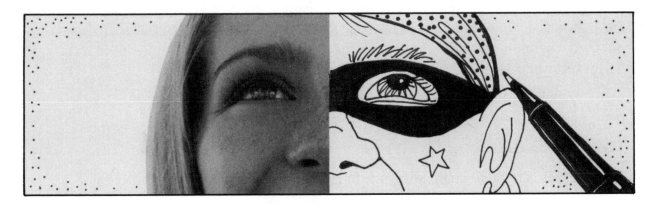

Alter Ego

There are several different approaches to this creative writing exercise. One interesting approach is to search magazines for full-page photos of a person. A full-face portrait, taken from the front, generally works best. Cut the page out of the magazine and then in half lengthwise, directly through the middle of the face. Paste one half of the cutout picture on a white piece of paper, such as copy paper. Students sketch and color their interpretation of what the other half of the face (the alter ego) looks like. Use the momentum of this brainstorming to guide the writer into a creative writing story.

Students can also use self-drawn portraits or have a neighbor draw them using these sketches as the basis for the cut-out alter ego. Famous people's photos can be found on the Internet, downloaded, and printed for this activity. The more famous the person pictured, the more fun can be had with the alter ego story. Be sure students visit the "Critics' Corner" and the "Construction Zone" as their stories develop.

TWISTS AND TURNS

Use this activity to spark students' interest in writing an autobiography.

Cubes

"Cubes" is an interesting and fun motivational game that takes a little prep work before class participation. We have included a character list (pages 46–48) for the class to use. If brainstorming characters has been taught, it will be fun to make up your own characters, descriptions, settings, and scenarios. Use the cube pattern on page 44 for your dice pieces. The dice that the students make are a hands-on introduction to the writing activity. Do not forget to encourage the students to develop the character, go through the writing steps, and to spend time completing art and the chosen publication method. Change a few things to personalize the activity to fit your needs!

PURPOSE:
- To be used as a starter or motivator
- Flexible use of characters
- Transitions
- Creative thinking and impromptu thought
- Cooperative learning exercise

CROSS-CURRICULAR USES:
- Applications to math or social studies
- The use of dice for random choices
- Brainstorming in many subjects

MATERIALS:
- White copy paper
- Scissors
- Glue stick
- Cube pattern (page 44)
- Colored pencils or markers
- Character list (pages 46–48) or brainstormed list

Motivational Creative Writing

Cubes

1. In small groups (three is a good number) have the students cut out and glue together three cubes.

2. Number two cubes like dice.

3. Color the third cube with six different colors, one for each side.

4. The colors represent the type of role the chosen character will play in the story.

STEP·BY·STEP

5. Each student rolls the three cubes; the numbers on the dice that match the number on the list are paired together and used in the story according to the color the third die has turned up.

   For example, a student rolling "snake eyes" would find character 11 (or 2) and use it according to the color of the side up on the die that has been rolled. (Character number 11 is "Helga the Horrible," and the color green, for example, represents the main character of the story.)

   The colors of the cubes can be labeled "Hero," "Villain," "Narrator," "Child," or "Victim," etc.

6. If a student rolls a 5 and a 2, they can choose between characters 52 or 25, or they could even add them together and choose character 7.

7. Once a student has rolled for two or three characters, they will have enough material to begin a story. Of course, you can also brainstorm settings and scenarios by adding a fourth die.

8. Each student will have their own set of characters and should write their names down as soon as they roll and land on a character. When characters have been selected, students write their rough draft.

9. Students, in groups of three, meet in the "Critics' Corner" to do the first editing, followed by a rewrite.

10. Select a method of publication—"The Comic Book" (pages 17–19), "Accordion Books" (pages 128–129), or "Package Deal" (pages 133–137).

11. Students work on the publication and present it at the "Construction Zone." Students make any last-minute changes or corrections and proceed to publishing the final product. Be sure to review "Tips for Art and the Finished Product" on page 151.

TWISTS AND TURNS

- Social studies: The colors and numbers on the cubes can represent various settings, people, important events, and dates in relation to the unit you are studying.

- Time line drill: Use one die for this activity. Divide a time line into six sections for the unit you are studying. Students roll the die and must tell all they know about what happened in the period of time that corresponds to the number on the die.

- Science: This can be used when studying the periodic table. Number the sides of the cubes to correspond with the periodic table.

Character Bingo

A fun twist to "Cubes" is playing a variation of "BINGO" using the board on page 45 and the Character List (pages 46–48). A letter W, R, I, T, or E has been assigned to each character on the list. These letters are used to represent the columns of a "BINGO" card. Students roll the dice until they earn a "Bingo!"

When bingo is achieved, the student must use those four or five characters in an original story. The colored die, rolled along with the numbered dice, decides what part each character will play in the story.

There is plenty of room for improvisation in this process, just make up a system in any way that seems logical. The results will be that the students will have either four or five characters with predetermined roles. Their next step is to develop the characters' personalities as they plug them into their creative writing stories.

PATTERN

Motivational Creative Writing

W R I T E

		FREE		

Green HERO	Red VILLAIN	Blue CHARACTER	Orange VICTIM	Purple NARRATOR

◆————————◆

Motivational Creative Writing

CUBES CHARACTER LIST

W

1. Wonder Girl
2. YokoLoko, Boy Samurai
3. Willie the Wanna' Be
4. Captain Quack
5. Moon Man
6. Super Mom
7. Dane the Brain
8. Sweety and Ruff the Wonder Dog
9. Ahab the Boat Captain
10. Couch Potato Man
11. Sumo Pig
12. Kangaroo Man
13. Chrome Dome from Stockholm
14. Ray-man the Shaman
15. Cookie Man
16. Super Babe
17. Ninja Shadow of Dankness
18. Myrtle the Turtle
19. Peaches the Hero Dog
20. Lady of Light

R

21. Rainbow Girl
22. Veggie Man
23. Chunky Chocolate
24. Lance-a-lot
25. Gibberish
26. X-Ray Man
27. I Spy
28. Fly Man
29. Red Horn
30. I Got Game Jane
31. Slick Chick
32. Moo Moo, the Wonder-Cow
33. Zip the Lip
34. Hot Zoot
35. Cookie Mom
36. Hot Chocolate
37. Micro Man
38. Wishy Washy
39. Mini Van Man
40. Zero the Hero

Motivational Creative Writing

CUBES CHARACTER LIST

I

41. Jump Back Jack

42. Dangaroo

43. Tigger Cat

44. Meller Yeller

45. Fang

46. Sweet Pea

47. Bones

48. Famous Ramous

49. Shank Man

50. Time Stopper

51. The Threesome: Madder, Hatter, and the Sadder

52. Rocket Boy

53. Red Beard the Pirate

54. The Swashbuckers

55. Moop the Snoop

56. Amazing Grace

57. Shuga Champion of Sweetness

58. The Dazzler

59. The Whisper

60. Shadow of Darkness

T

61. Lash the Whipper

62. Ice

63. Uncle Harry

64. Ugha the Cave Girl

65. Kasta Spell

66. Mojo Workin'

67. Granny a Go Go

68. Disco Dad

69. Artie the Artist

70. Bubba the Super Plumber

71. Ghetto Blaster

72. Scary Hairy

73. Super Cop Callahan

74. X-tra, X-tra

75. Smooch the Pooch

76. Captain Marbles

77. Leena the Hyena

78. Bad Brad

79. The Deamon Seaman

80. Jean the Machine

Motivational Creative Writing

E

81. Stinger the Super Bee

82. Tennis the Menace

83. ? Q-Girl ?

84. Super Snooper

85. Frick and Frack, always on opposite sides

86. Choco and Latte, Crime Fighters

87. Sub the Meaner, Substitute Nightmare

88. Swifty, the Fastest Talker Alive

89. Clyde the Camel, Hero of the Desert

90. YingYang, the Confuser

91. Flat Frank

92. Muddler the BeFuddler

93. Mighty Mary

94. Minnie Van Man

95. Guido the Guide

96. Peppy and Ronie, the Pizza Delivery Men

97. Doubles

98. Babble Lon

99. Mellow Fellow

100. Leisure Lee

Motivational Creative Writing

1 2 3—3 2 1 Switch

Using the computer creatively!

Incorporating technology is a wonderful way to excite students about writing exercises. This activity utilizes technology and movement, taking advantage of all the energy that middle grade students have. Students will develop techniques for flow and sequence using three-part stories.

PURPOSE:
- To promote flow and sequence in writing
- To promote clarity
- To respond to the thoughts of others

CROSS-CURRICULAR USES:
- Technology and keyboarding
- Problem solving
- Language arts activities: descriptive paragraphs, poems
- Social studies

MATERIALS:
- Computer lab or several computers
- Paper and pencil or pen

1. Pick a few topics or ideas as potential creative writing themes. Place each student at a computer (adjust the lesson plan to fit the number of usable computers). Allow students to sit quietly, brainstorming (silently) possible story scenarios on one of these topics, or brainstorm together as a class.

2. Each student then starts typing their thoughts for a story, trying to focus as closely on the topic as their creativity will allow. This first session is limited to the introduction, setting, character development, and beginning of the story.

3. Students write without interruption for ten minutes.

STEP·BY·STEP

4. Ring a bell or give a one-minute warning before time is up. The students try to bring the first part of the story to a logical stopping place.

5. Announce the time to switch, and the students stand and move to the computer on their left.

6. Now, each student reads what their predecessor has written as the first part of the story. Trying to keep to the theme, the student's new task is to write the middle part of that story.

7. Students write uninterrupted for ten minutes. Repeat the switching process at the end of the allotted time.

8. The same procedure is followed a third time, but now the students bring the story to a logical ending.

9. Make sure students get credit for each of the stories that they have helped write.

10. The stories should then be printed and shared aloud with the entire class.

11. Be sure students visit the "Critics' Corner" and the "Construction Zone" as their stories develop.

TWISTS AND TURNS

• This process can also be applied to a handwritten format.

• If you want to take the stories to the next level, publish them for display using the steps of the "Critics' Corner" for editing, and any of the formats in the Publishing section, such at the "Package Deal" (pages 133–137). Be sure to include the "Construction Zone" and to review the information on "Tips for Art and the Finished Product."

Dance Line

This motivational creative writing exercise combines the fast thinking of brainstorming, the flexibility of making transitions, and theories connecting the thinking process and movement. Finally, art and a little drama employ the rest of the creative senses.

As always, the writing steps must be followed during publication of the story that has been developed from the "Dance Line." This lesson draws from "musical chairs," but has a new and creative twist. A teacher designee will be in charge of starting and stopping the music (as if the class was playing musical chairs). Play some new and popular music that the students will enjoy. Be ready for a bunch of fun and a lot of movement, two essentials for learning in the middle grades.

PURPOSE:
- Making transitions
- Cooperative learning exercise
- Brainstorming exercise
- Identify and recall information

CROSS-CURRICULAR USES:
- Science: a unit on planets, animal phylums, or rocks and their properties
- Language arts: creative writing activities
- Social studies: people and places in various periods of history
- Review drill in all subject areas: math, science, social studies, music, health, family and consumer science
- Foreign language: vocabulary drills

MATERIALS:
- CD Player
- Current CDs
- A package of 5" x 7" index cards
- Supplies for the chosen publication method

Dance Line

1. Brainstorm a list of characters and settings. Write each character's name on an index card, and write each setting on an index card, until all of your characters and settings are copied on separate cards.

2. Have the class form two lines facing each other. The members of each line will have the same type of card. (Each student in line 1 will have a card with a character name; each member of line 2, the facing line, will have a separate card with a location written on it.)

3. When the music starts, the class will begin passing the cards to the left, continuing until the music stops.

4. When the music stops, each student imagines a quality of the subject of the card he or she is holding, and writes a note on the card detailing his or her thoughts. Each person trades cards with the student facing him or her. This will help in mixing the cards and keeping the momentum of the activity.

5. Students will read aloud (at whisper level) their newly acquired card, asking any questions for clarity. Clarifying notes must be written on the card.

6. Restart the music and repeat until each card is filled with brainstorming ideas.

7. To bring the "Dance Line" to a close, stop the music and reorganize the lines, with character card holders in one line, and scene or setting card holders in the opposite.

Motivational Creative Writing

8. Pair up the facing card holders. One should have a developed character card, and the other should have a scene or setting card. Both cards should contain recorded input from several different classmates.

9. Each pair collaborates on the rough draft of a story, using the two cards as guidelines for the setting and characters.

10. Share the rough draft in a modified "Critics' Corner."

11. Make revisions noted from the "Critics' Corner" process. It is important to include this step in order to feel comfortable with the flow and scope of the soon-to-be-published product.

12. Publish, using one of the several methods presented in this book. Make sure that there is another editing review in the "Construction Zone." After final revisions, students are ready to publish their work. At this point, if artwork is included, be sure to review the "Tips for Art and the Finished Product" (page 151).

TWISTS AND TURNS

- When organizing the lines, students can be alternated standing and kneeling. This method (called the "jigsaw") helps the students concentrate on the person across from them, and keeps them from being bothered by the conversations of their neighbors.

- Another way to use this activity is to write on the cards a famous person's name or a particular historical period or event. When the music stops, students are to list any information they know about the subject, adding new facts on each exchange. This can also be done orally, and has proven to be a great review in science, social studies, and for math concepts.

- This is a great activity to use as a vocabulary drill.

- Collect and reserve cards to use later in other ways, such as themes for new stories.

Cuneiform

This ancient form of writing was developed by the Sumerians.

We have formulated a motivational writing exercise based on cuneiform. The exercise is not only creative in its approach, but fosters the growth of problem-solving skills through the creation and use of a new language.

PURPOSE:

- To promote problem solving through language development
- Summarizing
- Clarity
- Decoding
- Accuracy and attention to detail
- Following directions
- Brainstorming

MATERIALS:

- Alphabet developed by your students (or you can use the one included on page 58)
- Play dough (recipe on page 55)
- Brown paper bags, cut into rectangles the size of students' writing
- Popsicle sticks with one end cut flat, or sticks that students find outside
- Poster paint—various shades of brown (Using a different shade for each of your classes will help you keep them separate when it is time to display the work and return projects to students.)

CROSS-CURRICULAR USES:

- Creative writing of a short story
- Social studies: write a sentence depicting the life of a Sumerian
- Language development

Several thousands of years before the birth of Christ, the first civilizations were emerging in the Middle East from the area known as the Fertile Crescent. The river valley of the Tigris and Euphrates was a prime area for the development of civilized societies and positive communication between peoples.

The greatest leader of the Sumerians, Hammurabi, realized the importance of writing thoughts and messages, and promoted the development of a written language for his people. His famous "Code of Hammurabi" is the set of laws carved in stone so that everyone in the land would have faith and understanding that these laws would not change as the whims of the lawmakers might desire.

The early Sumerians developed a written language with letters and symbols that could be pressed into damp clay using a flat stick; when the clay hardened, the text was preserved. This form of writing predates Egyptian writing and the use of papyrus. This early form of Sumerian writing is termed "cuneiform."

TWISTS AND TURNS

Share with other classes inter- or intra-school by scanning pictures of their clay tablets and sending them over the Internet.

Cooked Play Dough Recipe

1 cup flour	1 cup water
½ cup salt	1 tablespoon oil
2 teaspoons cream of tartar	1 teaspoon food coloring (optional)

Directions

1. Combine flour, salt, and cream of tarter in a saucepan.

2. Mix liquids and gradually stir them into the dry ingredients.

3. When mixture is smooth, cook over medium heat, stirring constantly until a ball forms.

   This is very pliable and long-lasting play dough. It is easily preserved in an airtight container.

Cuneiform

1. Discuss the beginning of written language, how and why it came about, and its impact on civilization.

2. Discuss the various early types of written language.

3. Have students individually develop their own alphabet using symbols for the letters and for some of the commonly used words and terms.

4. After looking over the students' work, have the class or a selected group of students combine the samples from everyone's work to come up with one set of alphabet and word or terms symbols that the entire class can use.

5. Students compose a sentence or short paragraph about the life of the Sumerians or early civilization and rewrite it using their new alphabet.

6. As a class, make some play dough or have several students bring in some from home. Divide the play dough into balls about the size of a large egg.

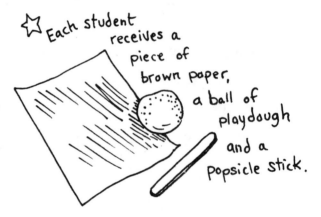

☆ Each student receives a piece of brown paper, a ball of playdough and a Popsicle stick.

7. Give each student a piece of brown paper bag and a play dough ball. On the back of the paper, have students write out their sentence using a fine point marker (so they do not forget what it says) and write their name on it.

On the other side, students flatten out the play dough on the paper to about ⅛" thick. This is their "clay tablet."

☆ Roll out the playdough. Flatten to ⅛"

Motivational Creative Writing

8. Using the flat end of a popsicle stick, students press in their story with the new symbol alphabet.

9. Let the "clay tablets" dry overnight and then lightly dry brush with the poster paint to give it an antique look. Be sure to get the paint in the grooves of the symbols so they are darker. Let dry.

10. Exchange "clay tablets" and have students pretend they are scribes and decipher each other's tablets. This is fun to do as a contest between classes.

Display tablets in the hallway along with the master alphabet—students enjoy the challenge of decoding the cuneiform.

Motivational Creative Writing

CUNEIFORM ALPHABET

This is a student-generated "early man" alphabet. Your students will have fun generating their own, or you can use this one.

Cyclone Stories

"Cyclone Stories" are short spiral stories written REALLY in the round. Using the prescribed writing process, students are taught to condense and compact their stories, to be precise, and to plan ahead! There is no room for rambling here. The stories are written on a spiral strip of paper that expands up and out as it exposes the artwork beneath the spiral. Students love to turn the paper around, or walk around the spiral (depending on the size) as they read the story aloud. This is an active and student-involved exercise in writing.

PURPOSE:
- To develop an understanding of compacting and summarizing
- To solve problems by planning ahead
- To promote fluency while editing

CROSS-CURRICULAR USES:
- Advisory activities
- Social studies historical events
- Famous people or places in science, history, or math

MATERIALS:
- Construction paper
- Glue sticks
- Scissors
- Colored pencils, fine-tip black markers or pens
- Cyclone pattern (page 62)

Cyclone Stories

1. Brainstorm the topic of the story after having shared some examples of finished products. Showing examples of the expected result is an important first step. Many students learn visually and grasp objectives quickly when they are presented clearly.

2. Brainstorm a setting. This will help students create a meaningful picture and plug into their drawing any character(s) that the story addresses.

3. Pass out the pattern for the "cyclone" found on page 62. This will be used for the rough draft and the published piece. Also, pass out the two sheets of final draft paper.

4. Write the rough draft on lined notebook paper.

STEP·BY·STEP

5. Students will share their stories with each other in the "Critics' Corner." Each will read another's story aloud, stopping when there is need for clarity. Author takes note and makes any needed changes (see page 117).

6. Students rewrite, counting words and spaces in order to fit the story on the cyclone. This problem solving is an important step in the overall process. Sometimes the student must write their story backwards, from the center outward, in order to make it fit on the pattern.

7. Take the production paper and trace the pattern onto it using the rough draft cyclone pattern.

8. At this point students can visit the "Construction Zone" (see page 115) and then transfer the corrected rough draft to the production paper. Use pencil and write lightly so that mistakes can be erased.

9. Using fine-tip black marking pens, trace over penciled-in story.

10. Cut out the cyclone, but not all the way to the edge of the paper. The cyclone must be framed by the uncut margins of the paper.

11. Lay the second sheet of paper under the cutout cyclone. Lightly trace the hole that would be opened when the cyclone spiral is extended.

12. Plan, draw, and color the picture that will fit under the spiral of the cyclone. Maintain the theme, ending, or characters of the story.

13. Glue the cyclone spiral on top of your picture so that it fits under the spiral hole. (A glue stick works best.)

14. Finish with pictures and designs around the edges of the Cyclone. Remember to color heavily, work large, color all of the paper, and outline in black marker or pen. See "Tips for Art and the Finished Product" (page 151).

☆ Write the rough draft of your story.

☆ Copy your story onto the cyclone pattern, first in pencil, then in marker.

☆ Cut on the line of the cyclone pattern.

☆ Lay a second sheet of paper under the cut pattern.

☆ Lightly trace the hole that will be opened when the spiral is extended.

☆ Draw your story picture.

☆ Glue the cyclone spiral on top of your drawing.

☆ Finish with pictures and designs.

Motivational Creative Writing

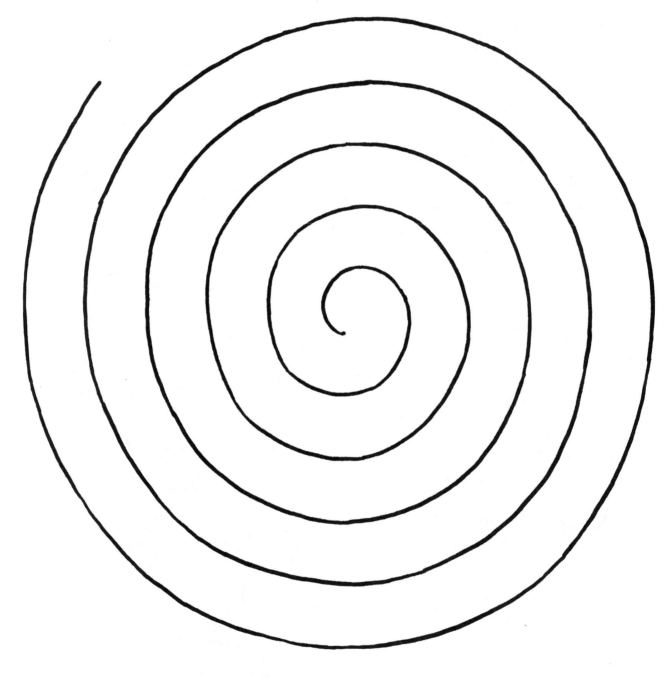

Motivational Creative Writing

Greek Vases

This activity can stand on its own or can be taught as an interdisciplinary activity combining mythology, language arts, social studies, and art. While studying and researching a unit on Ancient Greece, students design a vase using one of the six main Greek styles. Their drawings are to reflect an aspect of Ancient Greek life, their gods, myths and fables, Olympic games, or the wars of the time. Students attach to their vase a written explanation of the scene they chose to depict.

PURPOSE:
- Coordinating interdisciplinary studies
- Social studies research
- Displaying facts in an artistic and historically accurate manner

CROSS-CURRICULAR USES:
- Social studies: the study of Ancient Greece
- Reading and language arts: the study of mythology
- Art: art history lesson, pottery, figure drawing

MATERIALS:
- Examples of vase shapes and their uses (page 65)
- Black construction paper
- Orange or terra-cotta construction paper
- Black fine-tip markers
- Glue sticks

Greek Vases

1. For this particular creative writing lesson the class must be assigned research on Greek myths and legends along with the Greek gods. The art and the social studies parts of the lesson must be coordinated. The lesson can also be taught on its own and not presented as a cross-curricular activity.

STEP·BY·STEP

2. After researching their topics, students gather their information together, decide on the theme of their essay, and write the rough draft.

3. With the rough draft complete, students gather in the "Critics' Corner" to have their papers edited, following up with needed revision.

4. Students then select the shape of the vase they want to make and cut it out of black construction paper.

5. Depicting a part of their research or its theme, students draw a scene in the Greek fashion on a blank sheet of paper.

6. Cut the orange or terra-cotta construction paper to fit the section of the vase where the design will go. Transfer the pencil drawing to the construction paper, then outline it with a black marker.

7. Decorate the upper and bottom edges and the handles of the vase in the traditional fashion.

8. Mount the final report on either black or orange construction paper (or a combination of the two), and attach it to the completed vase. Present it in the "Construction Zone" for final editing.

9. Make any last editing changes and turn in the final project.

TWISTS AND TURNS

- These make great bulletin board displays.

- Mount the vases on stiff paper and cut them up for an "archeological dig."

- In cross-curricular applications, the pottery can actually be made of clay and painted.

- With a short explanation, this can also be done using drawings of Greek temples.

Motivational Creative Writing

GREEK POTTERY

◆

Functional design was the mark of Greek pottery. Once forms were proven suitable, they were seldom varied. A few basic shapes perfected in Athens were:

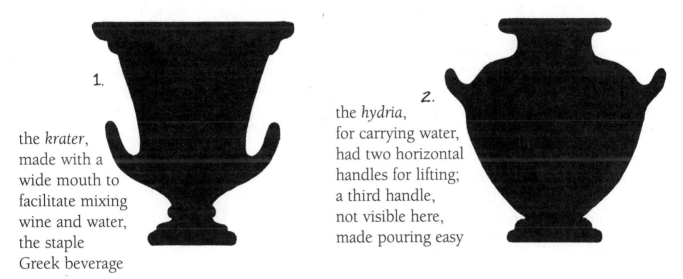

1. the *krater*, made with a wide mouth to facilitate mixing wine and water, the staple Greek beverage

2. the *hydria*, for carrying water, had two horizontal handles for lifting; a third handle, not visible here, made pouring easy

3. the *kylix*, a two-handled drinking cup

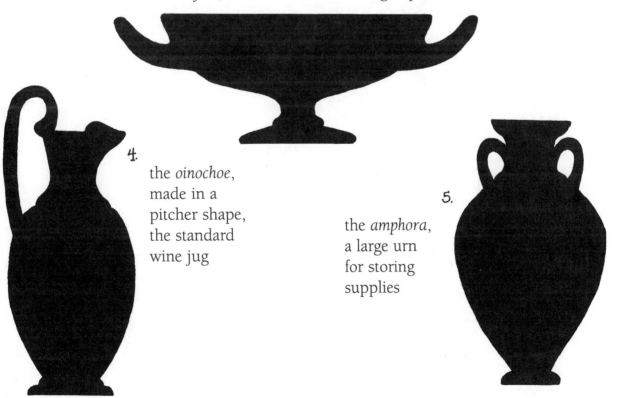

4. the *oinochoe*, made in a pitcher shape, the standard wine jug

5. the *amphora*, a large urn for storing supplies

Such vases established the Mediterranean supremacy of Athenian potters.

Motivational Creative Writing

Last Straw!

Motivational creative writing projects are successful when the end result is student ownership in the final product. The artwork incorporated in this project magnifies the pride students have in their end product. If comprehension is the requirement, there is no better way to reinforce the learning process than through one's own interpretive artwork. The learning pyramid shows that 80% of learning is through the seeing and doing processes. Student art displays the thought processes as an assignment is recalled. This is a powerful approach to writing and comprehension. "Last Straw!" combines these concepts with problem solving, comprehension, and clarity for a creative writing assignment in which the story's ending becomes its beginning!

PURPOSE:

- To develop an idea of tying the ending of a story to the beginning
- To understand that the end of a story used as the beginning might give insight into the theme of the story
- To promote fluency in a fun way
- To link problem solving to a writing activity
- To promote clarity and the whole of a story

CROSS-CURRICULAR USES:

- Examining historical events in social studies and science
- A kick-off for creative writing and language arts
- Good for exploratory classes

MATERIALS:

- Clear tape or a stapler
- Construction paper
- Scissors
- Many straws, shish-kabob sticks, or old Pick Up Sticks
- Colored pencils or markers
- A vase or container to hold the finished products

There are many different ways you could kick off this assignment, and you should determine what fits best with your group of students. What follows is just one of many different starters to this writing activity.

1. Brainstorm with the class a list of several different story endings. Or, use a teacher-generated list.

2. Cut out pieces of yellow paper in a wavy pattern. Each cutout should be about ¼ of a standard-size sheet. The wavy pattern should resemble a flag blowing in the wind.

STEP·BY·STEP

3. Recheck the ending of the story for spelling mistakes and or punctuation errors. Use a fine-tip marker to copy the ending on the cutout paper flag. (Or type this part, cut it out and glue it onto the wavy cutout.)

4. Using a stapler or clear tape, attach the edge of the flag to the straw. Roll the paper around the flag pole until it curls tightly around it.

5. Collect the finished straws and shuffle them up randomly. Then, have the students choose a straw from the collection and read it to themselves.

6. The students write a three-part story using the ending that is written on the flag as the beginning of their story. Follow up with the editing process.

7. Produce the final piece using the "Package Deal" (pages 133–137).

TWISTS AND TURNS

- Use this type of lesson with impromptu speeches in language arts.

- Modify the activity with flags that have the beginnings rather than the endings, and ending the story with the beginning.

- Make flags of different colors.

- Post facts for test questions and vocabulary words on the flags and use the flags for review drills. The student collecting the most correctly answered flags receives a reward.

LAST STRAW!

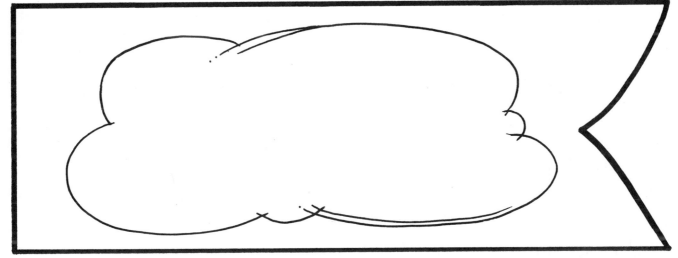

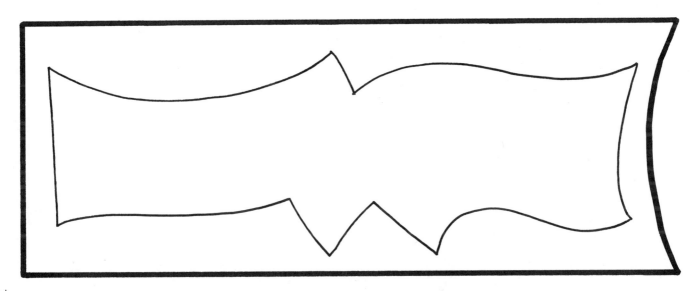

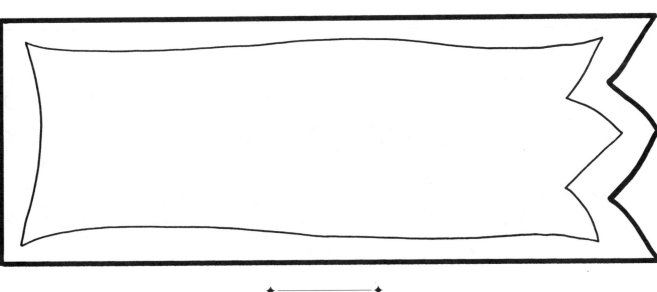

Motivational Creative Writing

The Pirate Ship Battle

"The Pirate Ship Battle" is a great quick write and a lot of fun to produce. This exercise in creative writing can be taught in one class period, with another period for publishing the final product in one of the formats presented. (The "Picture Frame" fits this project well.) There are several ways that you can use this piece, and it is especially well-suited for problem solving. "The Battle" and "The Rescue" (page 72) can also be included with the "Treasure Map" activity (see pages 73–75).

PURPOSE:
- A motivational starter for creative writing
- A tie-in for projects that have already been started

CROSS-CURRICULAR USES:
- The activity can be changed to fit many subjects, especially social studies and problem solving.

MATERIALS:
- White paper (8½" x 11")
- Scissors

Motivational Creative Writing

The Ship

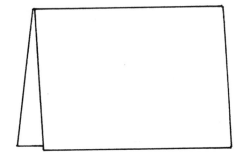

1. Fold a piece of white paper in half the "hamburger" way.

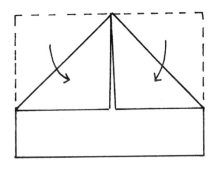

2. Fold two corners toward the middle of the paper so it makes a triangle.

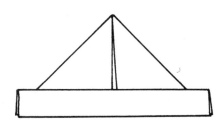

3. Fold each leftover strip up on either side.

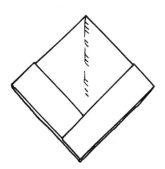

4. Holding the center of the base, gently pull the paper open, folding it into a diamond. Fold the ends of the side flaps over one another.

5. Pull carefully on the ends, and gently pull the sail up from the middle.

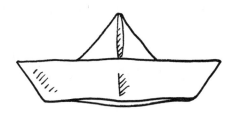

6. You should now have a paper boat with a sail sticking up.

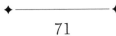

Motivational Creative Writing

The Battle

1. Students pair off pretending to engage in a mock sea battle with their partner.

2. Each student tears off a piece the bow, the stern, and the top of the sail as the battle rages.

3. As the ships sink, a miracle unfolds!

The Rescue

1. Unfold the boat and you will have a "life vest!"

2. Now, for the creative writing!

3. Brainstorm with the class possible scenarios for a quick-write story.

   a. Compose the story of the battle and the rescue.

   b. Write on the front and back of the "life vest."

   c. Share the stories in front of the class.

4. Publish the final draft with the "Picture Frame" (page 142) or any other method of displaying a finished product.

TWISTS AND TURNS

- Use this scenario to generate creative thought for problem solving.

- Take the project to a higher level of thinking by brainstorming how the person might survive and what kinds of hardships they might encounter.

Motivational Creative Writing

Treasure Map

This captivating activity challenges students to use their knowledge of directions and map-reading abilities while strengthening their descriptive writing skills. With the recent success of pirate movies and the timeless appeal of high-seas adventure, students will have a high interest in the activity. Studying the Caribbean and the history of pirates, along with the geography of their domain adds excitement to the lesson. Try to use actual longitude and latitude locations so that the imaginary treasure will be hidden in a real location that one could identify on an actual map.

PURPOSE:

- To provide a lesson in giving directions
- To reinforce map skills
- To use as a geography lesson
- To promote creative writing
- To use as a background for any "ancient" project or writing piece

CROSS-CURRICULAR USES:

- Geography lesson
- Science: writing about ancient astrologers, scientific theories, or scientific equipment
- Social studies: writing activity about ancient times

MATERIALS:

- Brown grocery bags or mailing paper
- Markers
- Pencils
- Atlas or social studies textbook

Treasure Map

1. Make a map with a paper bag by making it look like leather. Wrinkle and re-wrinkle the paper, until it begins feeling and looking like leather. The more the paper is handled, the softer and more leathery-feeling it will become!

2. On a separate sheet of paper, draw the rough draft of a map, marking latitude and longitude lines.

3. Choose a place anywhere from the Bahamas to Venezuela as a location for the buried treasure.

4. Draw the island on the map, in pencil first (with straight lines for longitude and latitude since it is a small map).

5. Decorate the map with (select a few): pirate ships, sea monsters, mermaids, the North Wind, a compass rose, or other typical map decorations.

6. Indicate the treasure on the map with an X.

The island or land mass should include some features to help someone find the hidden treasure, such as: palm trees, a mountain range, a pond, a fort, a harbor, a dock, a sunken ship, or a reef.

Motivational Creative Writing

7. Write a story that gives directions to the treasure and explains how it got there. Use the proper terms for land forms, directions, and measurement. Complete the "Critics' Corner" cycle with the story, making any necessary changes.

8. Now, write the story in pencil on the prepared brown paper, and go to the "Construction Zone" for the last editing.

9. For the final touch, ink in the story, writing each word in "capitals and dots"— starting and stopping at the end of each pen stroke (see below).

TWISTS AND TURNS

- This can be used for any writing activity dealing with history. An excellent example is a writing activity assigned after discussing the Black Death.

- Discuss the technique of writing with quill pens and how the letters would have a "blob" of ink where the pen was first set on the paper for each stroke and again at the end of the letter. This can be recreated now by putting a dot where the "blob" would be. This technique results in a realistic rendition of aged lettering.

Motivational Creative Writing

Entangled in the Web

This adventure into creative writing is a lesson with extremely high interest and focus. Middle grades students flourish when given the challenge of being "Entangled in the Web." The prerequisite for this lesson is access to computers with Internet capabilities, either at home or in the classroom, media center, or lab. Also, a teacher or computer-proficient student (or parent and community volunteers) must know the basics of MicroSoft PowerPoint. Most sixth through eighth graders will know how to navigate through PowerPoint, or you will have at least one or two students who can become "Ambassadors of Knowledge" to help teach the basics.

For this lesson, students will compose a creative writing project using pictures and video clips that are readily available on the Internet and/or the PowerPoint program itself. The challenge is to have the students pick a minimum of ten to fifteen slides, writing and presenting a PowerPoint presentation with clip art, downloadable art, and video. The final production (publication) takes place when the slide show is played and given constructive criticism by the class in a "Construction Zone" format. Make sure to have the class decide upon a rubric to use before beginning the project (see pages 155–159).

PURPOSE:

- To present varied and creative approaches to quality writing
- To familiarize the students with the use of the Internet
- To increase knowledge of computer programs and functions
- To stimulate creativity through a new writing medium
- To foster flexibility in the thought process

CROSS-CURRICULAR USES:

This writing activity has cross-curricular applications for every subject that is taught in the middle grades. Teachers in every subject area will be able to draw on the students' knowledge of PowerPoint and its integration with the Internet. Interested middle grades students will publish quality reports and well-done projects.

MATERIALS:

- Computers
- MicroSoft PowerPoint™ program
- Access to the Internet for a more varied degree of audio/visual resources
- It is nice to have recordable CDs in order to save large files and to preserve and share the presentations.
- A computer projector allows the whole class to enjoy the students' presentations.
- A digital camera can be incorporated into the lesson.

1. Students must develop a theme for their writing assignment. The theme can be:

    a. brainstormed by the class.

    b. assigned by the teacher.

    c. motivated by pictures viewed on the Web.

STEP·BY·STEP

2. Open the PowerPoint program to a new presentation.

3. Minimize the window.

4. Connect to the Internet and make a search for GIFS or animated GIFS. Select a site that allows use of their GIFS without cost.

5. Download GIFS or pictures appropriate to the lesson. Download the GIFS to a disc so that they are retrievable off-line.

6. Apply photos, pictures, GIFS, Animated GIFS, text, narration, color schemes, sound, and transitions to the slide show.

7. Present the slide show for constructive criticism from peers according to the "Critics' Corner" guidelines.

8. Make any final changes to the presentation and double check the rubric before proceeding to the "Construction Zone."

Motivational Creative Writing

TWISTS AND TURNS

- Students take "flip book" type slow motion pictures with a digital camera, putting them together with dialogue in a PowerPoint presentation.

- Model clay into figures and take pictures of them like a "Claymation" movie.

- Record voices into the PowerPoint, presenting the story as a narration.

- Write and act out an original play. Video clips can be included with the PowerPoint presentations.

- Use original student art and photograph it with a digital camera. Base the written story on the theme of the art. Apply to the PowerPoint show.

Freedom is a Gift

This motivational creative writing exercise is a one class period presentation that promotes self-examination of one's inner feelings. There are many possible variations to the basic format of "Freedom is a Gift," and the following is one that is dynamic in its impact.

PURPOSE:

- To increase awareness of the differences in freedom vs. captivity
- To visualize differences in body language and demeanor
- To teach proportion when drawing
- To promote empathy
- To compare and contrast

CROSS-CURRICULAR USES:

- This activity can be used in several different core and exploratory classes.
- School counselors can use this for character development.
- D. A. R. E. officers can teach this lesson in several different ways.
- Language arts writing activity
- Art activity on proportion, shading, and 3-dimensional drawing
- An applicable lesson for the advisory period

MATERIALS:

- Pictures of animals, collected from magazines or student-generated
- Black construction paper
- Assorted colored construction paper for mounting
- Scissors and glue or glue stick

Motivational Creative Writing

Gather a collection of foam cartoon masks of wild animals. (You can use large pictures of animals cut from magazine pages—*National Geographic* is a good resource. If you have the students sketch a picture of an animal, they can use encyclopedia pictures or items on the Internet as portrait models.) The students pick an animal mask to wear. Let them interact and have fun by making animal noises and motions. Brainstorm as a group the many and varied feelings that the animal might have, the locations where they may live in the wild, their surroundings, the weather, the ecology, food and resources, family and babies, protection, fears, their future, etc. "Future" is one of the key ideas to introduce when leading the students in brainstorming.

1. Ask the students to jot down bulleted statements of their thoughts about each item on the compiled list.

2. Have students sketch the face and shoulders of their animal. Their sketch should be a portrait-style picture, about as large as their own hand. Reserve the finished picture and bulleted statements for later use.

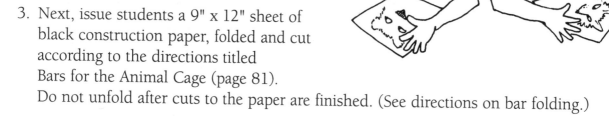

3. Next, issue students a 9" x 12" sheet of black construction paper, folded and cut according to the directions titled Bars for the Animal Cage (page 81). Do not unfold after cuts to the paper are finished. (See directions on bar folding.)

5. Each student should center the finished animal drawing on a working surface.

6. After they open the cutout construction paper bars, instruct students to place them overtop of their drawing (vertically, like bars on a cage). Immediately, ask the class to jot down their new feelings in bulleted statements.

7. Glue the bars over the top of the students' drawings.

8. Choose a writing lesson for the class.

9. Use the "Picture Frame" method for display. (See page 142.)

Motivational Creative Writing

Bars for the Animal Cage

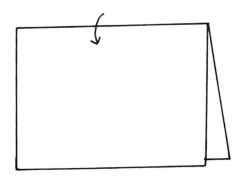

1. Get black 9" x 12" construction paper.

2. Fold paper in half the "hamburger" way.

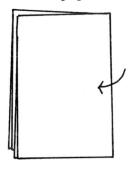

3. Fold in half again "hamburger" way, and then fold again a third time.

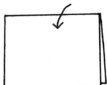

4. Fold up ¾" from the "open page" edge and crease well.

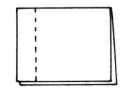

5. Unfold the ¾" flap and use the folded crease as a stopping point when cutting with scissors.

6. Cut from the folded edge to the crease ¾" from the open edges. Cut slices of about ¼". Be careful not to cut through the paper edge.

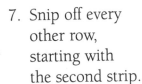

7. Snip off every other row, starting with the second strip.

8. When unfolded, you will have a set of bars to glue over the top of your animal drawing, placing it in a cage.

Motivational Creative Writing

Groucho

Everyone knows how it feels to be left out of the group. Sometimes this results from a mild form of discrimination, and at other times it is a more apparent form of being singled out! Here is a fun exercise that will demonstrate how character traits are most often assumed based on first impressions. This creative writing lesson will not only motivate the young writer, but open their eyes to some important observations about character development.

Before beginning, discuss as a class some of the issues surrounding group membership and "fitting in." Here are some questions to get you started:

- Have you ever gone to a party and found out that you were wearing an exact copy of a suit or dress that someone else was wearing? What kind of connections did you make with that person? Were you comfortable with the obviousness of the situation?
- Have you ever been on a team that dressed in the exact same uniform? How might it feel to be the only member of a team who was dressed in a different uniform? Would those team members wearing the same uniform seem more connected with their collective personality?
- Have you ever treated anyone differently because of some obvious trait that they had that you did not?
- Have you ever seen groups of people gravitate to each other because of their gender? Color? Color and gender? Age? Any other common trait?
- Do "identity like" groups work better together on a common task?

PURPOSE:
- To introduce likeness and unlikeness
- To aid in understanding others and their feelings
- To build character
- To put the writer in another's shoes
- To promote several approaches for reaching the same conclusion

Motivational Creative Writing

This is an energetic exercise in play and seriousness at the same time. A healthy personality involves being able to laugh at yourself, and there will definitely be a lot of laughter generated by this motivational writing exercise. No one is allowed to put on their glasses until all the Groucho sets are completed, and then everyone places them on their face at the same time! Get ready for some fun and controlled chaos. Once the class calms down, there are several motivational writing prompts that can be developed by the Groucho look-alikes. Some examples of prompts might be:

- Let the students wander about and see if they group up in any "common" arrangements. If they do, ask the class to stop and explain why they ordered themselves in a special way.

- What if everyone looked the same? Would it make a difference?

- If everyone looked alike, would fashion be important?

- How important would personality become if everyone looked alike?

- If everyone looked alike, how would you be able to show your individuality?

- Can being different be a good thing?

- Would looking alike change your views or associations?

CROSS-CURRICULAR USES:
- A character development lesson
- Exploring different societies in social studies
- The study of genetics

MATERIALS:
- Manila folders
- Scissors
- Glue stick
- Groucho pattern on page 84, or purchased Groucho nose and eyeglass sets

Identical sets of Groucho glasses, nose, and mustache are also easy and fun to make using the pattern on the following page.

Or, identical plastic sets can be purchased at a reasonable price.

Groucho

1. Cut out the pattern.

2. Lay the pattern over a manila folder so that the crease of the folder will be the center of the glasses.

3. Trace the pattern onto the folder. (Three Groucho sets can be produced from one manila folder.)

4. Cut out the glasses.

5. Color them with black marker.

6. Punch eye "peep" holes for pupils with a hole punch.

7. Cut slices in the mustache so that it looks hairy.

8. Shape the glasses to fit.

9. All of the glasses must be exactly the same!

10. Enjoy your new look!

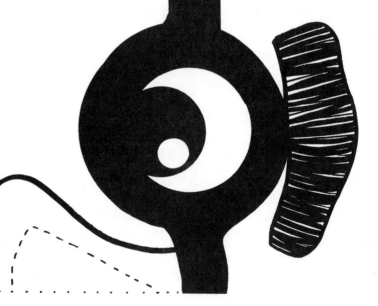

· PLACE ON FOLD ·

Ibis of Peace

"Ibis of Peace" combines the promotion of world peace with a graphic display of an origami ibis. A ceiling corner of the classroom can be reserved for wishes of peace by routinely adding a new ibis and its thoughts of peace. Each of the letters of the crane's name can be used for motivation to promote a thought of peace. For example:

I—I
B—Believe
I—It is
S—Sincere

Hang the ibis collection from the ceiling by thread or monofilament fishing line, and they will turn gently in the breeze. Display poems or essays with a peace theme written by students near the display of hanging "Ibis of Peace" cranes.

PURPOSE:

- To provide students with an opportunity to express feelings on world peace
- To use origami to promote the basic art needed for the construction of the ibis.
- Compact a concise message to one page
- Handwriting practice
- For promoting creative thought

CROSS-CURRICULAR USES:

- Language arts and creative writing
- Apply research techniques to the Internet or library.
- Counselors can use to help students express their feelings
- Art projects

MATERIALS:

- White paper
- Scissors
- Pencil
- Black fine-tip pen
- Fishing line or thread for hanging the finished product

Motivational Creative Writing

1. Using a piece of white paper, fold the corner to the opposite edge to make a square. Fold the extending flap over, creasing it firmly, and then either tear or cut it off on the crease. You should have a piece of paper about 8" square.

2. On the square piece of paper, copy an original, one-page thought on world peace. Use a pencil so that any mistakes can be erased.

3. On the reverse side of the paper, write the word PEACE four times across the top, and as many times as possible down the left-hand margin. Then, continue to write the word "PEACE" across the page until it is full. Trace the words in ink.

4. Now it is time to fold the ibis origami. There are several good books on origami that have directions for this and many other foldings. There are also several websites that have free origami folding directions. Or, use the directions found on pages 87–89.

5. After the cranes are folded and finished, monofilament line can be tied to the back of the birds and the line stapled or taped to the ceiling. A hole punch can make a hole for you to string the line through and tie it.

6. Do not forget that the writing component lends itself to some essays and poems. Include the "Critics' Corner" and "Construction Zone" in the editing and final draft processes. Get into the good habit of including the editing processes in the lesson.

Motivational Creative Writing

IBIS OF PEACE

① Start out with a square piece of paper.

② Fold diagonally, and unfold.

③ Fold opposite way diagonally, and unfold.

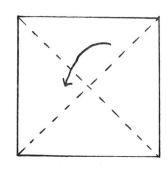

④ Fold in half, then fold in half the other direction and unfold.

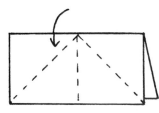

⑤ Take the rectangle by the sides and push them together.....

⑥ .... folding it into a diamond.

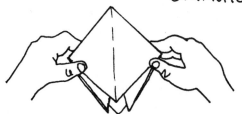

This is your base!

So far...
...so good!

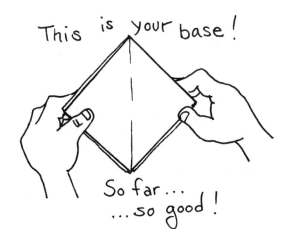

Motivational Creative Writing

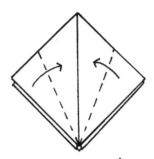

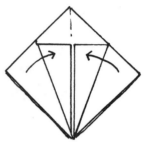

⑦ Take both sides of your top layer of the base and fold it towards the center.

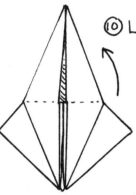

⑧ Turn your paper over and repeat. It should look like an ice·cream cone. Fold the top of the cone down and crease.

⑨ Open your folds, returning to your base shape.

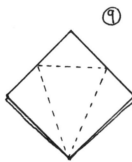

⑩ Lift open the top flap and press flat.

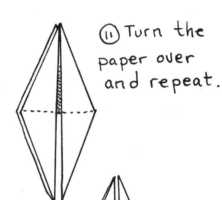

⑪ Turn the paper over and repeat.

⑫ Fold over the top left flap as if you were turning a page in a book...

IF YOU'VE GOTTEN THIS FAR... YOU'RE DOING GREAT! ☺

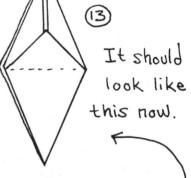

...then do the same with the reverse side.

⑬ It should look like this now.

Copyright ©2004 by Incentive Publications, Inc., Nashville, TN.

Motivational Creative Writing

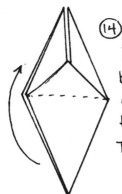

⑭ Fold the bottom point up to meet the top points. Turn over and repeat.

⑮ You should have a triangle like this.

⑯ Take hold of the two inner flaps...

...pulling them out to form the head and the tail. Crease firmly.

⑰ Fold down here to form a head ...

...and slightly curl out the wings.

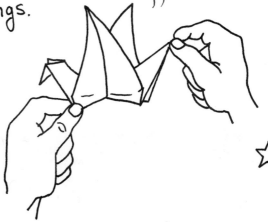

Your ibis is now complete!

☆ Hold the base of the neck and pull the tail — the wings will flap!! YAHOO!

89

Motivational Creative Writing

Group of 3

This activity utilizes both large and small groups. Students meet in groups of three to brainstorm a story line. The students act and react to the direction of the story line as each member of the group shares. This activity incorporates group work and develops class presentation skills and feelings of self-worth.

PURPOSE:
- To develop quick thinking skills
- To promote clarity
- To reinforce transitions
- To promote problem solving
- To work in a cooperative learning environment

CROSS-CURRICULAR USES:
- Foreign language and ESL dialogue
- Social studies reviews of lessons
- The scientific process
- Language arts oral and writing exercises

MATERIALS:
- Paper and pencil
- Three chairs
- CD player and some musical CDs
- Materials for the chosen publication method (pages 127–150)

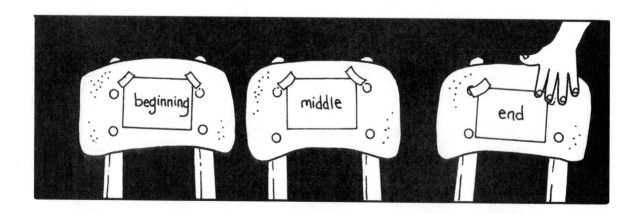

Motivational Creative Writing

1. Meet with the class in a large group and get them fired up about a creative writing subject. Wear something crazy or show a picture of a shocking character (anything to create some energy).

STEP·BY·STEP

2. Give several prompts, and then begin some large group "brainstorming."

3. Divide the large group into groups of three and instruct each of them to come up with a story idea, setting, and some characters.

4. After ten minutes or so, bring the large group back together.

5. Place three empty chairs in front of the group, and tag the chairs "Beginning," "Middle," and "End."

6. Call up each group of three, one at a time. Play music as the students walk around the chairs. When the music stops, the students have to sit in the chair that is closest to them (as in musical chairs), representing the beginning, the middle, or the end of the story. Each student must tell the part of the story that corresponds to the chair in which they are sitting. Each student builds on what the previous student has said.

7. After each member of the three has shared his or her part, the large group may ask two or three questions about the story that they do not understand. Remember, no "put downs!" This is a modified "Construction Zone," used before the "Critics' Corner."

8. After each group has shared their stories, their next task will be to write the rough draft of a story inspired by their own presentation. Have them keep in mind any questions the unclear parts produced. This can be done individually or by the group of three.

9. Assign a minimum of 175 words for the rough draft.

10. The students will bring their rough drafts to the "Critics' Corner." Because of its reverse order with the "Construction Zone," this is the final chance for editing.

11. In order to complete the stories, students must choose one of the publishing formats found on pages 128–150. Remember to refer to "Tips for Art and the Finished Product" (page 151).

TWISTS AND TURNS

Play musical chairs with a large group of students. Every time that three students are eliminated by the music, they become partners in a creative writing exercise. The winner is exempt from the story, but must develop the art for the story of his choice.

Patriotic American Flag

In recent years, the United States has experienced a reemergence of pride in the American way of life. Patriotism can manifest itself in many different feelings, thoughts, and actions. Challenging students to consider what America means to them is the perfect introduction for this motivational creative writing activity.

PURPOSE:

- To increase proper grammar usage
- To inspire the creative thought processes
- To promote planning
- To improve hand-eye coordination
- To demonstrate and practice art skills
- To develop problem solving
- To promote brainstorming

CROSS-CURRICULAR USES:

- Advisory activities
- Social studies historical events
- Famous American people or places in science, history, or math
- Famous American patriots
- Writing activity
- Grammar lesson

MATERIALS:

- Red and blue 9" x 12" construction paper
- 8½" x 11" white copy machine paper
- Fine-tip pen (black)
- Glue sticks
- Scissors
- #2 pencils

To begin this activity, display the American flag and ask the class to stand and say the "Pledge of Allegiance" aloud. Direct the students to pick out the nouns in the pledge and make a list of them. As a class, review the meanings of the nouns and how they apply to being patriotic. Discuss some other nouns that represent the American sentiments, such as: freedom, peace, liberty, democracy, spirit, courage, brotherhood, pride, etc. Why are these ideals important to Americans? What do they show about us as citizens? Using the motivation from the list of nouns and the class discussion, students write seven different sentences, each starting with one of their chosen patriotic nouns.

Students meet in the "Critics' Corner" to check for clarity and spelling.

Use the directions on pages 94–96 to lead the class in making their own reproductions of the American flag out of construction paper. On the white stripes on the back of the flag, each student writes his or her the patriotic sentences. Allow time for the students to share and display their work.

TWISTS AND TURNS

- Brainstorm famous patriotic Americans, places, and events. Students may select those that they would like to research and write about for this activity.

- Used the finished products as displays for patriotic American holidays, such as Memorial Day or President's Day.

- Research other countries with stripes on their flags, such as Greece and Indonesia.

Motivational Creative Writing

STEP·BY·STEP

Making the American Flag

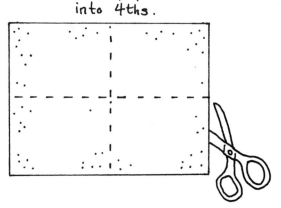

① cut blue paper into 4ths.

1. Divide the blue construction paper into fourths and cut. You will need only one ¼ piece of blue paper, so one sheet is enough for four students.

② Fold red paper in half...

2. Fold the red construction paper in half the "hot dog" way.

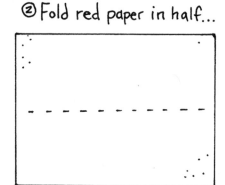

③ ...and in half again...

3. Divide it, and fold each half in half, and then those halves in half again. This should make sixteen sections. This might take some opening and refolding, so be patient. Make sure your folds are well-creased.

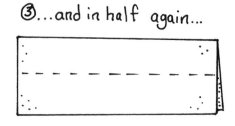

...and in half again...

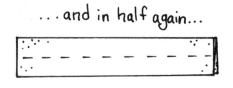

...and again.

Motivational Creative Writing

4. Cut off the last three sections, leaving thirteen.

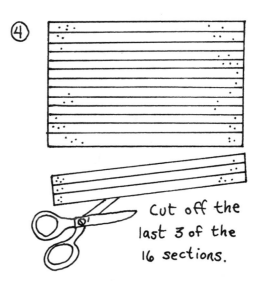

④

Cut off the last 3 of the 16 sections.

5. Fold the red paper the "hamburger" way.

⑤ Fold in half the "Hamburger" Way.

6. Cut on each fold, from the center of the paper (the crease), stopping about ¾" from the edge.

⑥ Cut on each section line.

7. Weave the piece of white paper in and out of the cuts on the red construction paper. At this point, the flag should have thirteen red and white stripes.

⑦ Weave the white paper through the red and ⑧ cut off the remaining white paper.

8. Cut off the white paper that extends past the flag, and reserve it for later use.

Motivational Creative Writing

9. Fit the scrap of blue paper into the proper position on the American flag. Trim if necessary.

10. Take the white paper scrap from step 8, and sketch (in pencil) the largest star that you can. Cut out the star and glue it to the middle of the flag's blue field.

11. Write the patriotic sentences on the white stripes of the flag. Share them aloud in front of class. Laminate and display.

Motivational Creative Writing

Star Ship Shuttle

"Star Ship Shuttle" combines three motivational projects that could each stand alone but are even more fun when combined into a single writing assignment. There is a lot of cooperative and collaborative interaction in this project, so be ready for the fun and the excitement that comes with it.

First the class collectively creates images of an alien character though a memory drill. Students draw their own mental visualization of the character, and this is followed with the rough draft of a 1-page, 3-part story. The activity continues as students build a space ship shuttle craft, hold a flight competition, and team up with a partner in order to write a new story using story parts created by others. Sound complicated? It isn't. But it is noisy, involved, and a lot of fun! With a little imagination, this exciting motivational process can be used in other subjects across the curriculum.

PURPOSE:

- To promote cooperative and collaborative learning
- To use memory drill as a learning tool
- To be flexible in the thought processes
- To use students' kinetic energy in a positive way

CROSS-CURRICULAR USES:

- This activity can be used in most any core and exploratory classes.
- In math, use the memory drill to help students remember math facts. The "spaceship" can be used for math problem solving.
- The memory drill is helpful when teaching biological classifications in science classes.
- In language arts, the activity is applicable as a creative writing activity and to practice writing transitional sentences or paragraphs.
- Use the "spaceship" with different parts of speech, and have students add new words after each flight.

The Memory Game

1. Arrange the group in a circle and give the following directions for "The Memory Game" (see also page 117).

STEP·BY·STEP

One student begins by describing a feature of an alien he or she has just encountered.

The second person in the circle must repeat the description of the first student's alien, and then add one feature of his or her own.

The third person in the circle repeats the descriptions of the first and second students, adding on his or her own description.

Continue this process all the way around the circle.

2. Students return to their desk to draw and color their own representation of the alien, according to these instructions (see page 101):

    a. Fold an 8½" x 11" sheet of paper in half the "hamburger" way.

    b. Draw the picture of the alien and trace it on the opposite side for a 2-sided drawing.

    c. Color both sides identically, and color heavily!

    d. Outline with a fine black marker.

    e. Cut out the drawing, leaving it connected at the fold.

    f. Put the picture aside for later use.

3. As a class, brainstorm different scenarios that the alien's story could take. Using these suggestions, each student must write a 3-part story.

4. Set up the "Critics' Corner" and edit (see page 111).

5. Students rewrite using their notes from the "Critics' Corner."

The Spaceship

1. Distribute the handout on page 102 to help guide students through this activity.

2. Students fold a piece of paper (8½" x 11") into thirds. Using the three sections as the beginning, middle, and end, students copy their rewritten story onto the folded paper.

STEP·BY·STEP

3. Instruct students to cut off the beginning section of the story and set aside the middle and ending (they will be used later).

4. Give each student a sheet of paper (8½" x 11") and a paper clip with which to build a "spaceship."

5. Using the pattern on page 103, students fold their "spaceship" paper airplanes, folding the beginning of their story into it. Students can individualize their spaceship with original drawings.

6. Encourage experimentation to find the ideal placement of the paper clip to maximize its weight and balance.

7. Fold the cutout alien character until only its head will stick out of the spaceship when inserted into the center fold of the plane. Insert the alien pilot into the finished and colored spaceship.

8. Place the paper clip on the front of the spaceship, in order to hold the pilot in and to give the aircraft some weight and balance.

9. Take the class into the hallway and assign each student a number. Have the class practice flight according to number, and suggest any modification that might help increase the length of the flight.

Motivational Creative Writing

10. Each student gets two practice flights in order to make their final adjustments.

11. At the end of the third and final flight, leave the planes where they land in order to record the longest flight and shortest flight (and those that come in between).

12. In reverse order according to number (the last student to fly their plane gets first choice), allow the students to select another student's spaceship to use for the next part of the project. After everyone has chosen a spaceship, make sure that no one has their own.

13. Allow the class to open up the spaceship and discover the beginning of the story that is hidden in the fold. Students plug in the newly found beginning into the middle and ending of their story, making any adjustments needed in order to have a smooth transition.

14. Type the story (condensing it if needed) so it will fit on one sheet of paper.

15. Give each student a 9" x 16" sheet of colored paper with which to construct a frame for the project (see page 142). Mount the finished story in the frame.

16. Creatively place the captured alien onto the picture frame and secure it with glue.

17. Both authors will take credit for both of the stories and the illustrations. (For example, Written by Bobby and Jill; Illustrated by Jill.)

The Alien Visitor

After finishing the alien's description as a class, it is time to draw your own unique image of the extraterrestrial while it is fresh in your mind!

Fold a sheet of copy paper in half the "hamburger" way.

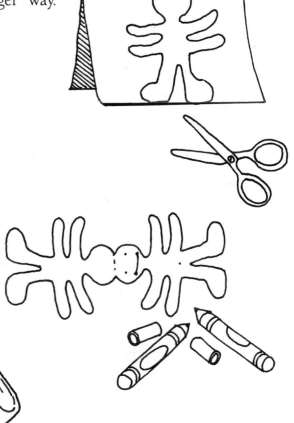

Draw the alien, and add a mirror image on the back side of the paper.

Cut out the picture; it will be the same on the front and back.

Outline the alien in black marking pen and color in darkly with colored pencils (the same on both sides).

Glue him together, and he is ready to pilot his spaceship!

Motivational Creative Writing

The Alien Spaceship

BUILDING THE SHUTTLE:

STEP·BY·STEP

1. Fold the "Alien Spaceship" using the pattern on page 103.

2. Decorate the spaceship as you think any alien might.

3. Place the alien character cutout in the shuttle.

4. Move the alien back and forth in order to scientifically determine the best weight-to-flight ratio.

5. Place a paper clip on the nose of the shuttle for flight control.

FLYING THE SHUTTLE:

STEP·BY·STEP

1. All participants get only two test flights (in order to make weight and flight adjustments).

2. After the third and final flight, the shuttle will be left where it lands.

3. After all the shuttles have flown (and crashed), swapping begins. The last student to fly his or her shuttle gets first choice of a new shuttle.

After all shuttles have been swapped, add the middle and end of your rough draft to the beginning of your new alien's story. After using the "Critics' Corner" and "Construction Zone," the final copy can be published. Using the "Picture Frame" is a good technique for publishing the final product.

Motivational Creative Writing

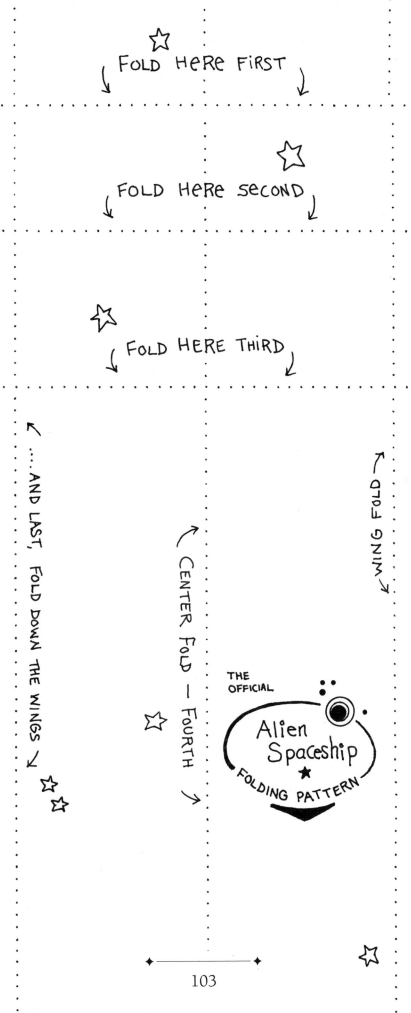

FOLD HERE FIRST

FOLD HERE SECOND

FOLD HERE THIRD

WING FOLD

CENTER FOLD — FOURTH

...AND LAST, FOLD DOWN THE WINGS

THE OFFICIAL
Alien
Spaceship
FOLDING PATTERN

Motivational Creative Writing

METHODS

- What Good Creative Writing Looks Like
- Things to Remember When Setting the Mood for Your Story
- Brainstorming Worksheet
- The Critics' Corner
- From Brainstorm to Story Line
- Story Line—Parts 1 and 2
- The Construction Zone
- Modeling by Talking and Thinking Aloud
- The Memory Game
- Graphic Organizers and Brainstorming
- The Spider Web
- Made-Up Creative Words
- Creative Lettering
- "It's the Plumber"
- Plumb a Phone: An Editing Tool

✦—What Good Creative Writing Looks Like—✦

Some studies show that the criteria for good writing should be the same for all grade levels, without taking into consideration the age and level of the student. While there are problems with following this philosophy in the classroom, it is a good principle. However, teachers should be flexible—planning assignments through class discussion and agreeing on what is to be scored, as well as on the indicator of success (the rubric). Good creative writing takes many shapes and forms, especially when creative publishing is involved; however, the meat of the writing will always display the traits that allow good communication through the writing process. A great way to have the class understand what good creative writing looks like is to model an example of an exceptional creative writing product. Slowly read the piece aloud, and with your guidance, the class can compile a list of things that made the story fun and interesting to read. You will be surprised how accurate these indicators can be. Here is a list of indicators as agreed upon by a 6th grade class while critiquing a student's creative writing comic book.

- "Set the scene well."
- "You could hear the 'person to person' in the story."
- "I felt connected or felt that I was in the book as an observer."
- "I could see and feel the story as it unfolded."
- "The story went smoothly from page to page."
- "The plot was easy to follow."
- "Characters were explained well."
- "There were a variety of ways used to describe."
- "Great dialogue!"
- "Funny made up words and names"
- "The verb tenses agreed."
- "There was a logical beginning, middle, and end."
- "One part followed the other well."
- "Followed the rubric very well"
- "Nice look to the presentation"
- "Good mental imagery"
- "Words were spelled right and the sentences were correct."

Indicators such as these can be used to make up a rubric for a specific writing assignment. All 17 could be place on the "3-10 Rubric" as its top set of goals. However, this would be cumbersome and appear as too difficult to achieve. We suggest that you combine those items that are similar and shorten the list to one that is manageable ("The Best and Easiest Rubric," page 157). Always model good examples of the finished product in order for students to have a clearer understanding of the lesson's goals.

✦———✦

Strong Verbs Always Help!

Do not get tired of sharing ideas and involving your classes in the planning of a creative writing exercise. There are many "tricks of the trade" that good writers employ in their published pieces. Many of the stories that are well written have been crafted through the use of colorful words, a thesaurus, and utilizing strong verbs. Brainstorm with your class a list of strong verbs and have the students keep the list in their writing portfolio. Revisit the list from time to time and add newly rediscovered strong verbs.

Here is a partial list of strong verbs that has been brainstormed in a 7th grade classroom.

analyze	digest	investigate	reveal
annoy	disclose	link	review
apply	divulge	melt	rhyme
brainstorm	edit	memorize	scream
cancel	embellish	navigate	search
capture	embody	partake	separate
charm	epitomize	participate	shave
communicate	eradicate	persuade	shrivel
connive	exaggerate	ponder	stifle
consume	exemplify	probe	suppress
converse	explain	prod	tell
critique	express	query	trigger
decipher	exterminate	quote	understand
decorate	extreme	recapitulate	urge
design	identify	reconcile	visualize
detect	imagine	reflect	warn
devour	infuriate	regurgitate	
diagnose	interpret	remark	

Of course this is a partial list, meant to be a starter list for the class to use and add to throughout the year. Word cards can be made and displayed around the room as visual reminders of verbs that could be used in order to get a strong point over to the readers. Encourage students to use a thesaurus to find alternate verbs to the ones chosen that also carry strong meanings. It is amazing how fast this list grows as students incorporate strong verbs into the writing process. When listing the strong verbs, do not put them in alphabetical order or in linear columns, so that when searching for a verb the writer will have to visually scan the page, therefore mentally absorbing visuals of other strong verbs. This is also a wonderful way to build vocabulary.

Tools

You need the right tools in order to build a great creative writing story!

In order to expedite the creative writing process, open the creative writers' toolbox and get out the important tools needed to complete the writing task. Keep all of the supplies handy. Make sure there is a good dictionary handy, and a guide to punctuation and grammar (such as a textbook or workbook). Make sure the writer has a few sharpened pencils with good erasers, his or her creative writing portfolio, and a good supply of paper. Having all of the tools at hand will insure that the writer has the opportunity for success. They will not have to get up to look for the right supplies, and instead they can stay focused on the writing assignment. If art is involved in publishing the creative writing piece, then all of the supplies needed to complete the assignment should be at hand also.

Self-Editing

Have students self-edit for one type of error at a time. Do not overload them by asking the student editor to do a multi-tasked editing. Instead, have them focus on one area at a time. Do not think of it as revising, but consider it "revisiting" the story.

Remember that you do not have to start a "revisit" at the same place every time; you could start the revisiting process any place in the written piece. For example, you might ask the student to edit for strong verbs. If the student feels like replacing an existing verb with one that is stronger, he or she is not correcting a mistake, just building a better story. If the classroom set-up accommodates it, an editing center is a great idea.

Place a computer in the editing center and have the students type their stories. Allow them to use computer program tools to find synonyms and expand their word usage. Learning alternate words is a means for students to build a better vocabulary.

THINGS TO REMEMBER WHEN
SETTING THE MOOD FOR YOUR STORY

———— ◆ ————

THE SCENE is important for establishing the mood. In most cases, it will determine how the reader interprets the feelings intended by the author.

THE BEGINNING is the hook that catches the reader's interest and hopefully carries the interest to the conclusion of the story.

THE MIDDLE develops all of the characters and the problems of the plot. This is where all of the important action is.

See if you can capture the "essence" of the characters.
- Build the qualities of the characters
- Describe their values
- Size and looks
- Dress and demeanor
- Moods—shy, quiet, smart, etc.
- Sounds, smells, body language
- What does the character want?
  What is his or her role in story?
- What is the character feeling?
- What is different or out of the ordinary
  about the character?
- What does the character like or dislike?
- Support the descriptions with examples.

THE END must support the main idea of the story and bring the story to a logical resolution.

◆ ———— ◆

Motivational Creative Writing

BRAINSTORMING WORKSHEET

INSTRUCTIONS:

Write down as many ideas as you can in a 5-minute time period. Remember that no idea is a bad idea during "brainstorming." Do not be concerned with spelling or handwriting—yet. The idea behind the brainstorm is to create a list of characters, scenes or location, themes, story ideas, endings, etc.

HERO	SUPERPOWER
VILLAINS	**POWERS**
OTHER CHARACTERS	
SCENES OF ACTION—LOCATION	**CREATIVE WORDS**
RESULTS	**ENDINGS**

110

Motivational Creative Writing

Critics' Corner

The "Critics' Corner" is an effective way for students to share their prewriting with their peers and come away with some positive ideas on how to improve the final copy. The rules are simple and effective.

1. Students form groups of three and separate themselves from the rest of the class. They can sit in a corner of the room or in the hallway, etc.

2. Each group of three elects a member of the group to serve as the "anchor." This student is in charge of the group and keeping the members on task.

3. The students exchange their prewrites (story line) so that no one has their own.

4. The students silently read the story line to themselves.

5. Next, each student reads the story line aloud to the group and interviews the author. The reader stops to ask questions of the author about anything that is not clear or that the reader does not understand. At this time, the neutral member of the group also has the opportunity for some positive input.

6. The author is required to take note of the questions and make a record of the parts that are not clear to the reader.

7. Everyone in the group of three goes through the same process until all story lines have been shared.

8. Each author interview ends with at least three positive statements from the reader before the next interview begins.

9. When all three interviews are completed, the group members return to their seats and make the improvements to their own story lines.

FROM BRAINSTORM TO STORY LINE

Fold a large piece of white construction paper into fourths, then label each block (front and back side of paper) with one of the headings listed below. Each block (see pages 113–114) represents a single page in the story. Use this as a guide in writing your rough draft (the "prewrite" or "story line"). Using the edited brainstorming ideas, write and sketch the following layout into the appropriate blocks. Remember that the content of each block will transfer to a page in the completed work.

COVER AND TITLE This page should also include an action picture of the main character and a hint of the location. Try to fill the page with your work.

SETTING THE SCENE This page is the introduction to the theme, characters, location, and the meaning of the "made-up words" in the story.

The BEGINNING PAGE gets the story rolling. Make sure that the potential reader has a clear picture in mind of the characters and the direction of the story.

The MIDDLE PAGE contains the action and focus of the story. It gets the reader interested.

MORE OF THE MIDDLE PAGE is the real "meat" of the story. The reader should have an understanding of the characters and the direction the story is headed! It contains a lot of action and movement.

TOWARDS THE END On this page, the action and focus of the story should be logically moving toward an ending.

LOGICAL ENDING PAGE, where the hero wins! Use a funny ending, but remember to keep it in line with the theme of the story. It should not leave the reader confused.

BACK PAGE (about the author) includes your name, class, teacher, school, location, the date, and some information about the project and you.

STORY LINE (PART ONE)

COVER AND TITLE	SET THE SCENE
action picture, main character, location	theme, characters, and scene; definition of "made-up" words

BEGINNING	MIDDLE
	the action and focus of the story

Motivational Creative Writing

STORY LINE (PART TWO)

MORE OF THE MIDDLE	HEADING TOWARD THE END
(the real "meat" of the story) The reader should have an understanding of the characters and the direction of the story.	The action and focus of the story should be logically moving toward a resolution.
LOGICAL ENDING The hero wins! Keep the ending in line with the theme of the story, and have fun with it.	**BACK PAGE (ABOUT THE AUTHOR)** name, class, teacher, school, location, date; about the author; about this writing project

You can fold a piece of notebook paper in half twice to achieve the "8-Block Prewrite" format (four squares on each side).

Motivational Creative Writing

Construction Zone

The last chance to build it right!

The "Construction Zone" differs somewhat from the "Critics' Corner" yet accomplishes the same results. However, this stage gives the final copy its last-chance editing before production. This process is perhaps the most important step in order to produce a quality finished piece.

At the start of this process, students have a final copy that is not 100% complete, but well on its way. Much of their book might still be in the "penciled-in" stage. The "Construction Zone" should clarify any difficult-to-understand parts of the story, as well as give the author some pointers for making the final project more attractive.

This is a whole-class undertaking, and each author shares his or her project for peer review "center stage" in front of class. Of course, the teacher oversees this operation and applies the "no put downs" rule for comments. Most people, young people included, are sensitive about criticism (especially when it is directed toward their own creativity). Many times an author sees things differently than the audience. Remind your class of this before beginning the "Construction Zone," and set an example for your students of sensitivity to others' feelings.

Randomly choose a recorder, assigned to take notes, for each presentation. After the presentation, the recorder will read the noted suggestions aloud to the class and give the notes to the presenter. The random choice of recorders keeps everyone engaged.

If there are significant improvements offered for a project, the author may wish to make the improvements on a separate sheet of paper and then cut and paste the changes to their final project.

A good guideline to go by is that if the author must explain the story or the art to his or her classmates, constructive changes usually can be made.

◆—Modeling by Talking and Thinking Aloud—◆

When presenting any subject, the teacher should model the directions, and at the same time communicate their thoughts aloud. (What you are telling yourself mentally is what you should be saying out loud.) Confusing? Not really. Just maintain a steady flow of conversation that focuses on what you are teaching and the methods that you want to explain. Continue your steady stream of dialogue. Do not worry about making a mistake in the directions; if you correct your mistakes, your listeners will learn from them.

The key to this process is speaking your thoughts out loud! This will help you understand why some of the techniques are easy and others are difficult for your class to follow. Movement and hand and facial gestures are a must in your "talking and thinking aloud." Hand and facial gestures are "hooks" that learners can use in order to remember the fact related to the gesture. Movement is an essential ingredient for learning, and should be used often.

The Memory Game

This is a really fun memory drill that the teacher can apply to several topics across the curriculum. In the "Star Ship Shuttle" activity (pages 97–103), "The Memory Game" is used to begin an "alien" story, but that is just one of its possible uses. Everyone has to pay close attention and concentrate on not only what is being said, but also who is speaking and what expression he or she might be using.

1. Gather the class into a circle and have them get perfectly quiet.

STEP·BY·STEP

2. Make up the beginning to a story, as simple as a trip to the grocery store, or as exciting as a African safari or a time travel adventure.

3. Here is where the class gets involved. One at a time, each member of the circle adds an item or description to the story. After the first student adds their creation, the second student repeats what the first person said aloud and add a new part to the story. Each student in the circle starts with the first description, and lists each addition.

4. When the last student has given their description, the class returns to their desk and draws a detailed depiction of the story including every part that has been described. Students color their final drawing, trace the drawing with a fine black marker and cut out the picture.

5. Pin all of the pictures onto a bulletin board and discuss their likenesses and differences.

6. The creative writing juices ought to be flowing, so assign the completion of the corresponding story. The artwork is already finished!

"The Memory Game" is great for cross-curricular studies when items must be memorized and in order!

Motivational Creative Writing

Graphic Organizers and Brainstorming

One of the greatest obstacles that both young and experienced writers must overcome is the task of collecting their thought and ideas in a clear and useful form. There are many types and styles of graphic organizers that would work to help prepare the writer for an assignment. Graphic organizers encourage creative thought and build the foundation for a great story! The organizer on page 119 is a Spider Web, with twists and turns that plug in thought and momentum. Items necessary for sequence and flow are prewritten on the organizer. Change it in any way to fit your needs.

Students are able to understand expectations when their thoughts are outlined and recorded in an orderly and constructive manner. The flow and connections are much clearer, and organization skills can be transferred to their own thoughts. By bringing clarity to the forefront, students can get an overall picture of their thoughts, more than just a mental "snapshot."

Teachers can help students organize their thoughts and make constructive criticism. Being critical of a student's thoughts at this point does not seem to have any negative impact on the his or her thought process and brainstorming flow.

Use the graphic organizer provided to get started. It may be necessary to reproduce an enlarged copy of the organizer so that students have more room to write. In the "Story Theme" circle, the writer tells the plot. On the connecting lines, students write the relationships between characters. A short paragraph, for the story flow, goes in the spaces labeled the "Beginning," "Towards Middle," "Middle," "Towards End," and "Logical Ending." Bulleted statements rather than one-word entries work the best. This "Spider Web" does wonders for students, driving their creative engines toward a great story!

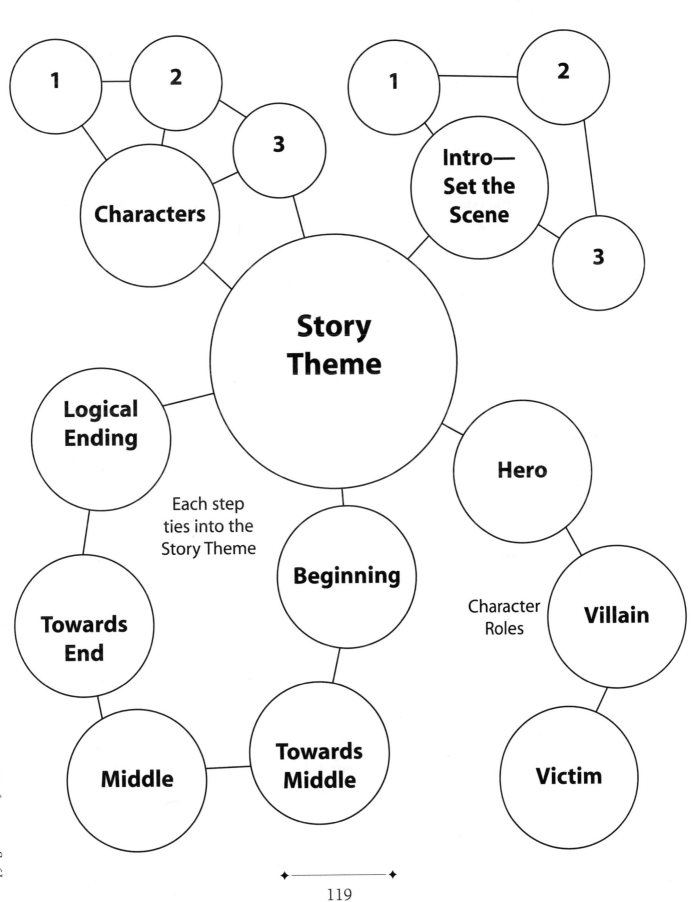

Motivational Creative Writing

Made-Up Creative Words

For action words, character names, or sound words!

Vary this presentation to fit your style and needs.

1. Produce several sets of some vowels and consonants out of card stock, and laminate them.

2. Shuffle and deal out the cards face down on each student's desk, two or three letter cards on each desk.

3. Choose seven students to bring a letter of their choice to the front of the class.

4. Without showing the card to the class, the chosen students pick up their letters and stand in front of the class.

5. Facing the class, the students will flip over the letters on the count of three, revealing their choices.

6. Next, the group of seven has 30 seconds to invent a creative word. They change places, holding the letters in front of them, until they agree on a word. Also, they can trade one letter for a vowel IF they can persuade someone in the audience to trade with them!

7. After the word is agreed upon, the group of seven has one minute to decide on the word's pronunciation and definition, and to use it in a sentence. To liven things up, play music or have the students hum a tune each time there is a waiting period.

    EXAMPLE:

    GAFLAP: (noun) a loud and funny noise created when two flaps slap each other; (adj.) loud and funny.

8. The entire class will write down the creative word, definition, and usage, and must insert several of these words into their next story.

9. Using the creative lettering techniques on page 121, cut out the words and post them, along with their definitions, around the classroom.

Creative Lettering

Making the Letters

1. Project alphabet transparencies onto colored construction paper.

2. Tilt the projector at different angles in order to distort the letters.

3. Trace the outline of the lettering.

4. Cut out the letters and laminate them.

5. Post the new "creative" words around the room.

Laminating Made Easy

1. Buy clear plastic shelf paper.

2. Cut the pattern a little larger than the piece you want to cover. (There are cutting guidelines provided on the backing.)

3. Peel the backing off, but not all the way.

4. Press the plastic on your letter, rolling the backing off as go. Trim any excess.

"It's the Plumber!"

"It's the Plumber!" is a wonderful and inventive tool to promote clarity, sentence and story flow, sequencing, voice, ownership, and editing. This is a unique and fun way to motivate your students to share their creative writing stories with a classmate, with editing and understanding as a goal. You will not believe how constructive this technique will become!

First read the following story about a plumber, a parrot, and a single woman.

Not so long ago there lived a single woman who had some plumbing problems that needed attention in a hurry. The woman had a very busy schedule and wanted to call a plumber to come and fix her leaky sink, but needed to fit the worker into a fairly restricted time schedule. She telephoned a local plumber and explained to him her time frame and the short window of opportunity. The plumber agreed that he would be at her apartment at 5:00 o'clock sharp that very day. She had made an important appointment at the dentist for 6:00 o'clock and explained the possible conflict to the plumber. "Not a problem," replied the plumber, and he asked for her address and apartment number.

The lady had only one pet, a parrot that lived with her and was her friend and companion. She loved the parrot so much that she spent hours trying to teach it to talk, so that the parrot could keep her better company. The only thing the parrot ever learned to say was "Who is it?" which he learned by listening to the lady ask that same question through the door each time someone knocked on it.

By a quarter 'til six, the plumber had not yet shown up at her apartment. Her dentist appointment was too important to break, so she decided to give up and reschedule him for another day. The lady checked around the apartment to make sure her parrot was comfortable and then left for the dentist appointment.

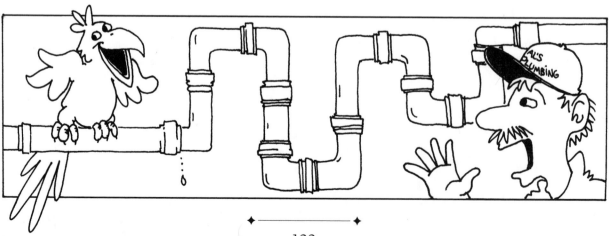

Motivational Creative Writing

She had been gone just five minutes when the plumber showed up at her apartment and proceeded to knock on her door.

"Who is it?" screeched the parrot.

"It's the plumber, I've come to fix the sink," the plumber replied from the other side of the door.

"Who is it?" screeched the parrot again.

Red-faced and louder, the man replied, "IT'S THE PLUMBER, I'VE COME TO FIX THE SINK!"

"Who is it?" screeched the parrot again.

Red-faced and popping the buttons at the neck of his shirt, he hollered, "IT'S THE PLUMBER, I'VE COME TO FIX THE SINK!"

"Who is it?" screeched the parrot once more.

Completely infuriated, the plumber screamed at the top of his voice, "IT'S THE PLUMBER, I'VE COME TO FIX THE SINK!" After that outburst, the plumber grabbed his heart, gasped, and fell over in front of the door, dead.

Within minutes the woman returned to her apartment only to find a dead man on her steps. She screamed "Oh my! There is a dead man at my door. Who is it?"

From inside the apartment the reply came, "It's the plumber, he came to fix the sink!"

Epilogue

The woman learned that the parrot was deaf in one ear and if she made him concentrate by whispering in his good ear, he learned new words much more quickly. The parrot is now reading the local 5:00 o'clock news. The woman has opened up a special school to teach parrots to listen and speak through the "whisper" technique.

Motivational Creative Writing

Plumb a Phone

Do you agree that in this story what was needed was better communication between parties? Clarity and understanding was certainly at a low point! Now enters the Plumb a Phone. The Plumb a Phone is a magnificent tool to be used individually or in pairs. This unique learning device is simple, effective, and cheap! Following these simple instructions will allow you to duplicate this highly effective communication tool. The instructions are as follows:

Go to the hardware store.
You will need:

    2 90-degree PVC fittings

    1 45 degree PVC fitting

    1 4" straight PVC tube

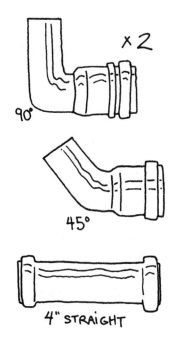

Fit the pieces together, without glue to still allow for adjustments.

It should look like this:

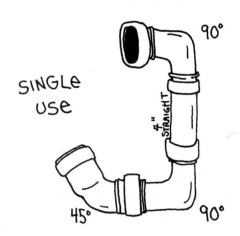

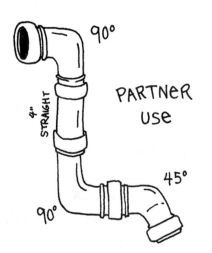

Motivational Creative Writing

Plumb a Phone

The Plumb a Phone is one of the greatest editing tools that we have ever discovered. It is simple and effective, and students look forward to using it. When a student has a prewritten first draft of any writing assignment that needs to be reviewed, the writer reads the story at a whisper level to him- or herself. Any issues of understanding, clarity, flow, sequencing, subject matter, theme, and connections become evident as the reader reads the story to him or herself. Clarity revisions must be addressed at this point, and editing will become a natural part of the student's writing.

Not gluing the PVC fittings together will allow for adjustments and use by one student or a pair. When using a partner-listener, editing guidelines must be followed. Use an agreed upon rubric to check on the progress of the piece, but the listener must always end the critique with two or more positive comments. The writer must address those items discussed with the listener, using the critique to improve his or her story.

The Plumb a Phone can be used across the curriculum and is especially well suited to use when clarity, flow, and sequence is being stressed. Use the technique for math when students need to memorize facts, practice oral reports, enunciating words and phrases in foreign languages, vocabulary drills, memorizing parts in a play, self-editing any written assignment, proofreading reports before considering the assignment complete.

Maintain the cleanliness of the Plumb a Phone by wiping the mouthpiece with a tissue, both before and after use. Antiseptic wipes and an occasional spray disinfectant is also a good idea. In fact, they are dishwasher safe, making it easy to insure their "germ free" status.

Motivational Creative Writing

PUBLISHING

- Accordion Books

- To Make a Book

- Package Deal

- On the Ball

- Picture Frame

- The Box

- Starburst

- Tips for Art and the Finished Product

Accordion Books

This is an attractive way to publish and show off student writing, be it a creative story, science project, or social studies report. It is quick and easy and looks oh-so-great!

MATERIALS:

- Colored poster board or tag board
- Ribbon—two pieces about 6" longer than the book is wide
- White construction paper

PROCEDURE:

1. Decide on the size and shape of book you want to make, and cut two pieces of poster or tag board. These will be the front and back covers.

2. Decorate the covers, including the title and a drawing.

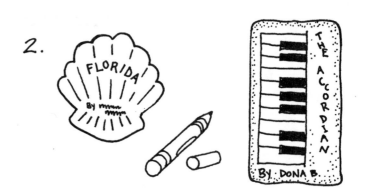

3. Cut long strips of construction paper ½" shorter in height than the cover pieces. The length of the construction paper will depend upon the length of the report. Two or more pieces may be needed if it is a long story.

4. Fold the paper accordion-style to fit the size of the front and back covers.

5. Once the paper is folded, determine the placement of the report or story and the art on each of the folded pages. Keep in mind the front and back flaps will be glued to the covers and will not be used as a space for writing or art.

6. Transfer the report to the accordion-folded paper. The story or report can be done on the paper itself or typed to fit the folded pages and pasted in place. Include the artwork at this point.

7. Now it is time to make the book. To tie the book shut, glue a strip of ribbon on the inside of the front and back covers. The ribbons should extend about 3" on both sides of the covers. Next, glue the accordion-folded reports in place. Tie the ribbons together to close the book.

Motivational Creative Writing

To Make a Book

Most any writing activity can be published in a book format after it has been edited. This is an easy process; just follow the steps outlined on the following pages.

When the steps are completed, the result is a premade blank comic book! The pages are ready for the student to apply the final edited story and the final art. Students tend to draw small, but large and simple drawings have better results.

Remind students to draw and write lightly in pencil, then go back over in colored pencil and add ink outlining. Or, vary this process by typing the dialogue and then cutting and pasting it in the book. Draw finished art on separate pieces of paper, and then cut and paste them into the book. Do not forget to make it colorful!

Laminate the cover. Share and display the finished products. Students and teachers alike will be proud of these creations.

130

1. Select a large piece of white paper, about flip chart size. You may want to use a scrap piece of paper for your first try.

2. Fold it in half ("hamburger" way).

3. Fold the paper in half again ("hamburger" way).

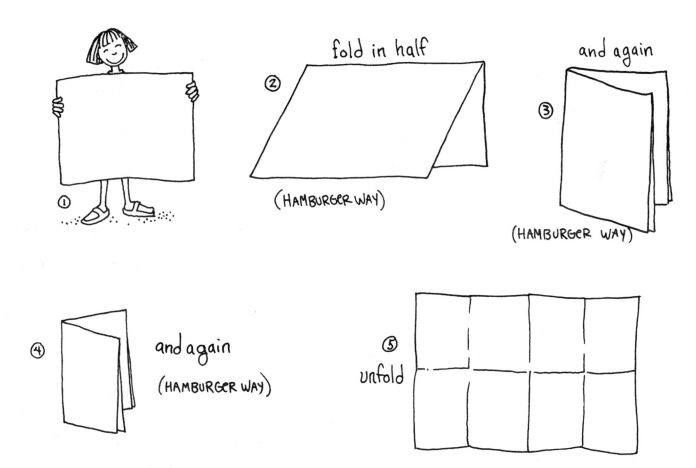

4. Fold it in half for the third time ("hamburger" way).

5. Unfold. This should make 8 large blocks on each side of the paper.

Motivational Creative Writing

To Make a Book

6. Refold again, as in step 2.

7. Holding the paper with the fold toward you, cut away from yourself along the center crease line, halfway to the opposite edge.

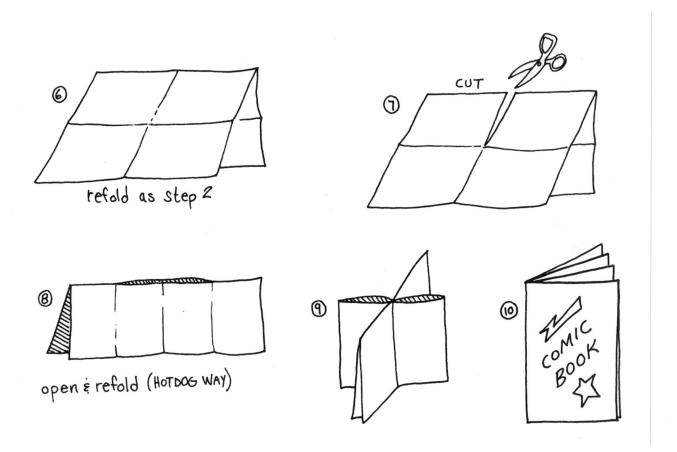

8. Unfold, and fold it in half ("hot dog" way).

9. Holding both ends, push the ends slowly toward each other to form what appears to be a "plus" sign when viewed from the edge.

10. Without any changes, fold the paper into an eight-page booklet. No staples should be required!

Motivational Creative Writing

Package Deal

"Package Deal" is one of the most versatile booklets we have ever come across. It is not complicated, yet produces an interesting and quality published piece. Brainstorm the different uses for this booklet, for it can be created quickly and adapted to many different ideas with great success. The basic booklet offers itself up to the artistic creativity of the author. Each unique "Package Deal" brings pride to its creator.

PURPOSE:

- To promote problem solving by organizing and planning ahead
- To encourage clarity
- To demonstrate compacting
- To practice developing the different parts of a story

MATERIALS:

- Scissors
- Glue sticks
- 1 sheet of 12" x 18" colored construction paper
- 1 sheet of 12" x 18" white flip chart paper
- A piece of yarn or ribbon about 36" long

Motivational Creative Writing

TWISTS AND TURNS

This is a wonderful and high-interest publication that lends itself to a multitude of uses. Here are just a few.

- Poetry showcase

- Famous person report

- Science experiment report

- A student play

- Steps to a mathematical problem

- Math formulas

- Menu or recipe packet

- Short story

- Study notes

- Young author's book

- Autograph booklet

- Greeting card

- Comic strip

Also, students can decorate the outer cover in a variety of ways in order to achieve individualized "packages."

- Use decorative punches on the fold where the ribbon is attached and insert contrasting colored paper to show off and highlight the colors.

- Consider decorating the package cover with the theme of the essay or story.

- Use colored ribbons, beads, feathers, leaves, dried flowers, etc.

PACKAGE DEAL

STEP·BY·STEP

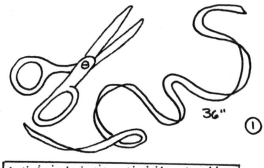

36" ①

1. Gather your materials.

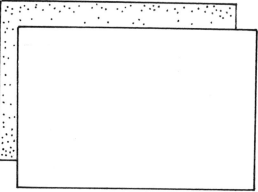

2. Cut the first piece of colored paper in half the "hot dog" way.

②

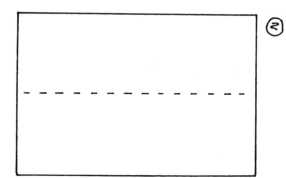

3. Fold the white piece of paper into thirds in both directions (4" folds the width of the paper, and 6" folds the length) so you will have nine rectangles when opened.

③

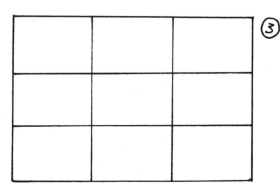

Motivational Creative Writing

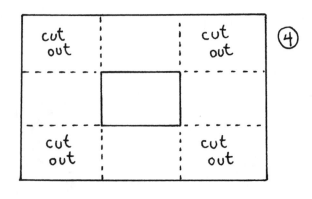

4. Cut the four corner rectangles away from the nine folds. This should form a cross of five rectangles.

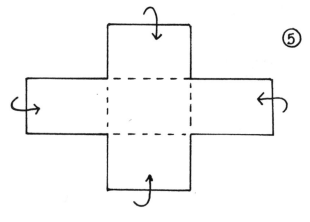

5. Fold the cross into a booklet by folding each leaf on top of the center rectangle.

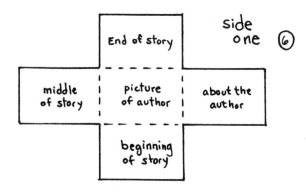

6. Transfer the edited rough draft to the appropriate pages.

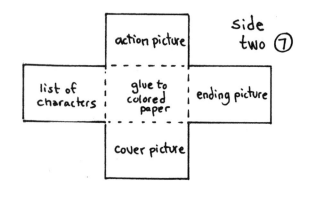

7. Transfer your art to the pages. Remember to refer to "Tips for Art and the Finished Product."

Motivational Creative Writing

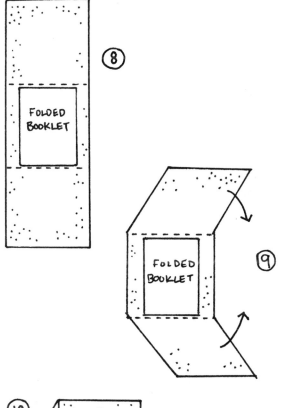

8. Now lay the folded booklet in the center of one of the 6" x 18" strips of colored paper.

9. Take the bottom of the colored paper and fold it up over the top of the white booklet. Then take the top piece and fold it down, covering the first fold.

10. Open up the top fold, and turn down the top edge about one inch and fold a sharp crease.

11. Use a paper punch to punch a hole through the doubled thickness, about ¼" from the folded edge.

12. Glue the booklet onto the center of the colored paper.

13. Attach the yarn through the punched hole, and tie the covering flaps.

On the Ball!

Combine this paper model of the world and a creative writing assignment and the result will be both eye-catching and informative. The art and paper construction is a fun and an interesting project in itself, and the production method of the ball or "globe" can be a teaching tool for both math and art teachers alike.

The actual ball is a 12-sided globe made of pentagon-shaped paper cutouts that are glued together. A sphere-like shape will naturally start to take form as the cutout pentagons are attached to each other. The mathematical term for the geometric ball is a *dodecahedron*. Each pentagon "face" on the globe is a stage for the student's creative writing and artwork.

The finished product can be displayed in several ways, but hanging each by a piece of monofilament fishing line one of the best. This unique publication technique lends itself to a host of cross-curricular instruction and is a surefire way to motivate!

PURPOSE:

- To showcase any cross-curricular report or research project
- To promote motivational publications
- To inspire creativity
- To teach planning and editing in a unique format
- To show the importance of planning ahead

CROSS-CURRICULAR USES:

- Social studies reports and projects
- Teaching geography
- Math: a geometry teaching tool
- Art: a 3-dimensional project

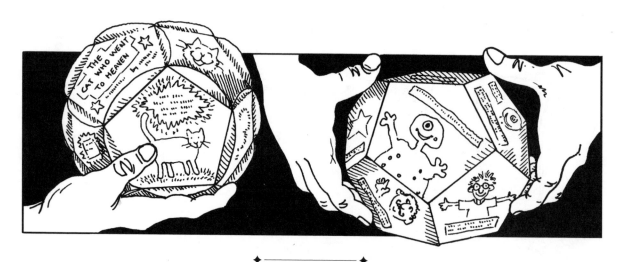

Motivational Creative Writing

MATERIALS:
- Pattern on page 141
- Construction paper or copy paper
- Art supplies: scissors, glue stick, stapler, colored pencils, black fine-tip marking pen, and some monofilament fishing line

1. Gather together the needed supplies, and get started! There are many different ways to start this motivational creative writing project. This is just an example using a social studies lesson.

STEP·BY·STEP

2. Have the class research a famous person in history or a historical event.

3. The student writes the creative writing story or historical report and take the rough draft to "Critics' Corner" for constructive criticism.

4. Revisit the rough draft and make any needed adjustments.

5. Cut out the pentagon-shaped faces of the globe using the pattern on page 141.

6. The next task is to preplan the placement of the story and the pictures on the pentagon-shaped faces of the globe.

7. Fold the edges of the cutouts along the dotted line of the pattern.

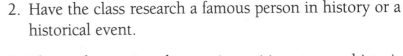

☆ You will need 12 circles to make your globe.

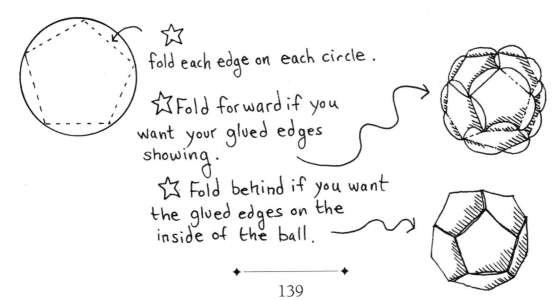

☆ fold each edge on each circle.

☆ Fold forward if you want your glued edges showing.

☆ Fold behind if you want the glued edges on the inside of the ball.

Motivational Creative Writing

8. Glue and staple the pentagon-shaped cutouts together using a glue stick and stapler. The stapler is used to staple the pieces together after they are glued, in order to hold the sections together as the glue dries so that students can continue working.

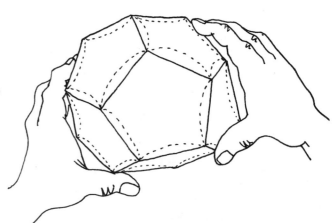

☆ Glue and staple all pieces together.

9. A naturally formed globe will begin to take shape as the cutout pentagons are attached to each other.

10. Before gluing down the art and edited text, run the project through the "Construction Zone" for clarity and flow.

11. The artwork should be in its finished state before being glued to the globe, for it is difficult to write or draw on the globe itself.

12. Remember to review "Tips for Art and the Finished Product" on page 151.

13. Staple a piece of monofilament fishing line to the top of the globe and display by hanging it from the ceiling.

TWISTS AND TURNS

• Reduce the size of the pattern to make three different sizes of balls. Do not glue the last panel of the large ball on all five sides. Glue down only one flap of the last panel and you will be able to open up the ball and expose the hollow center. Construct a smaller ball that will fit inside the larger ball, and then a then a third ball that will fit inside the second. The beginning, middle, and end of a story can be written on the panels of each ball.

• Physical education: create a model of a soccer ball, and write the rules on the blank panels.

• Using your imagination, depict a face on the shape of the ball. Just add ears and hair, a hat and eyes, a nose, and a mouth to create a character that can be used to help develop a story.

• Lines of longitude and latitude, the equator, the poles, the continents, and the oceans can be drawn on the ball and a geography lesson becomes creative!

Motivational Creative Writing

Motivational Creative Writing

Picture Frame

"Picture Frame" is a simple yet effective way to showcase written medium or art products that are one page in length. For example, use this format to display a poem or short story, a drawing or portrait, short reports or book reports, and informational documents. Supplies that are easily found and easy-to-follow instructions make this a useful and productive timesaver.

1. The written work or drawing can be any size, but you must have colored construction paper that is several inches larger than the drawing.

2. Place the writing or drawing in the center of a large piece of colored construction paper.

3. Measure equal margins of construction paper surrounding the piece that is to be showcased by the frame.

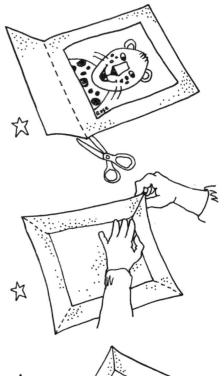

4. Cut off any colored construction paper that does not match the other sides of the frame.

5. Place the showcase piece in the center of the framed paper, and make small pencil marks at its edges.

6. Fold and crease construction paper in the exact outline of the showcased piece, but not all the way out to the edge of the colored paper.

7. Fold a line from the squared corner creases to the corners of the colored paper. This makes a 45-degree fold from the border fold to the outside corners of the construction paper.

8. The construction paper naturally takes the shape of a picture frame, and you can mount the showcase piece into it.

The Box

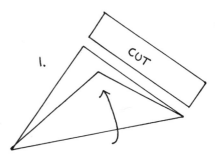

Use this folded paper box as part of the "Put a Lid on It!" activity, as a container for any creative writing piece, or just as a unique, 3-dimensional art project.

1. Fold a sheet of paper into a perfect square. Cut off any excess paper, and reserve the scrap for later use.

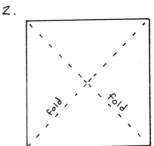

2. Fold the square from corner to corner in both directions to make an X. Sharpen the crease.

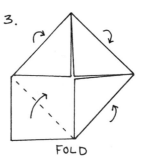

3. Fold all four corners of the square into the center, reducing the size of the square by half. Make sharp creases.

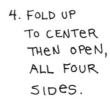

4. Now fold the straight edges into sharp straight folds using the center of the X as a measuring point for the folds. Fold each edge into the center, open, and repeat on all sides.

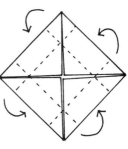

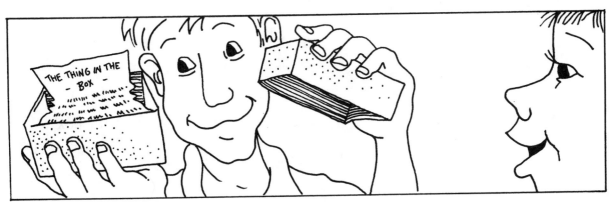

Motivational Creative Writing

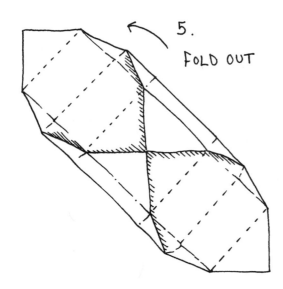

5. **FOLD OUT**

5. Fold the edges of the paper up until it looks as if it is taking the shape of a box. Then pull or fold out one of the pointed ends in the middle of the box-in-progress.

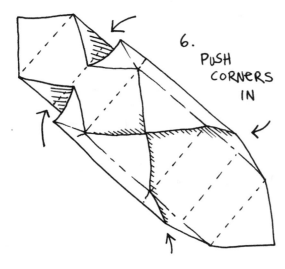

6. **PUSH CORNERS IN**

6. Push the creased corners in toward the center of the box-in-progress.

7. **FOLD OVER**

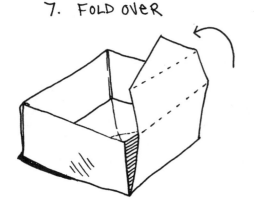

7. Fold the pointed flap over toward the center of the box and tuck it in. Have some patience at this stage, for it will take a little extra tucking, folding, and creasing for the box to have a crisp look.

8. Recrease and sharpen the edges. Repeat on the opposite side.

9. In order to make a lid for the box, fold the straight folds $\frac{1}{16}$" short of the center point as described in step 4.

Motivational Creative Writing

Starburst

"Starburst" is a great-looking finished product that can be adapted to many different assignments. A beautiful star shape unfolds as the the finished booklet opens. The 3-D star can be tied open with a ribbon and hung like a Christmas tree decoration. Students will have a ball folding and gluing the pages of their story together, and then watching it magically fold up into an interesting book cover. It will be hard for more creative students to stop making stars and stories of many different sizes, or just folding decorative paper stars. The project can be taught as a small group creative writing collaboration or used for an individual publication.

PURPOSE:
- To promote fluency in a fun way!
- To provide a writing activity linked to problem solving
- To provide a platform that promotes clarity
- To convey meaning, comprehension, and key points
- To use compaction and condensing
- To promote planning
- To promote brainstorming and creativity

CROSS-CURRICULAR USES:
- Showcase poetry
- Famous person report
- Science experiment report
- A student play
- Autograph booklet
- Greeting card
- Comic strip
- Mini-research reports
- Book reports

MATERIALS:
- Assorted colors of construction paper
- Tagboard for front and back covers
- Scissors
- Glue stick or white glue
- Ribbon

Motivational Creative Writing

This is another format that uses folding and geometric shapes to create a fanciful and unique display for a creative writing assignment or a project from any area of the curriculum.

1. Once the writing projects have undergone an initial edit in the "Critics' Corner," have the students choose the paper they wish to use and instruct the class in how to fold and glue the star rays together in order to have a completed starburst. (See pages 148–150.)

2. The students must plan how to edit their story to fit it, along with its art, to the rays. They must solve this sequence and order problem and know which pages to to glue to the covers in order to leave them blank.

3. Transfer the corrected rough draft to the folded rays of the star paper. Use pencil and write lightly so that mistakes can be erased.

4. Students may have to rewrite and count words and spaces in order to fit the rays of the paper star. This is problem solving, an important step in the overall process for an attractive finished look.

5. Plan, draw, and color pictures that will fit under the rays of the star. Illustrate the theme, the ending, or characters of the story.

6. Glue the covers on top of the folded paper star. The star will fold into a square, and a front and back cover can be made out of tagboard and decorated with art that carries out the theme and characters of the story.

Remember to color heavily, fill the page with your work, and outline everything in black fine-tip marking pen.

Motivational Creative Writing

TWISTS AND TURNS

- To make a book, cut a piece of tag board or other firm paper for the front and back covers, and glue to the first and last set of glued-together squares. Students write the title and illustrate the front cover and add an "About the Author" to the back cover.

- They can be used individually to showcase drawings and poems.

- This is an interesting way to display definitions for a particular unit.

- Social Studies: Write Chinese characters on the top triangle and the English translation on the bottom triangle.

- Math: Use with the study of angles and geometric shapes.

Motivational Creative Writing

STARBURST

This 3-dimensional form can be used individually or as a fold-out star with four sections making a book. It is the most striking when assembled using different colors of construction paper.

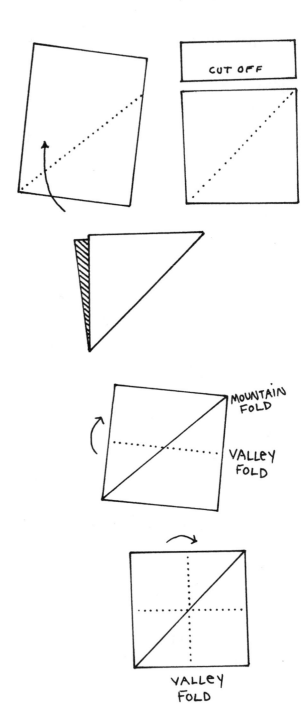

1. Fold one corner of paper to the opposite edge. Cut off the excess paper.

2. You now have a folded triangle. Set in the crease firmly along the fold line.

3. Place the paper on the table in front of you so the crease is up, forming a mountain. Now fold in half the "hamburger" way to form a valley.

4. Rotate the paper so the valley is perpendicular to you, and fold it in half again the "hamburger" way.

Motivational Creative Writing

STARBURST

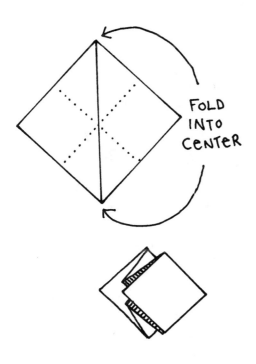

FOLD
INTO
CENTER

5. Hold the paper with both hands, with your thumbs on the sections without a crease. Bring the two sections together. This will cause the other two corners to fold into the center.

6. Do this four times, using a different color of paper for each piece.

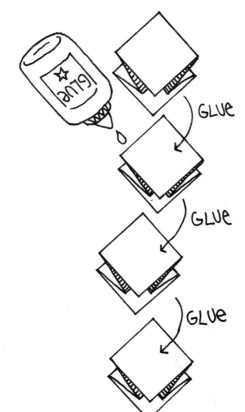

GLUE

GLUE

GLUE

7. Glue the four uncreased squares together, one in line with the other, remembering to keep the center fold in the same position for all of them.

8. Arrange the work so that it is in a logical sequence. Remember that all writing or typing should be done so that the words can be placed properly on the paper that will be cut out and glued into position on the starburst.

Motivational Creative Writing

STARBURST

STARBURST BOOK DIAGRAM

Showcase Panel:
- BLANK
- SHOWCASE THE AUTHOR
- ABOUT THE AUTHOR
- PICTURE OF THE AUTHOR
- BLANK

Ending Panel:
- PICTURE
- THE ENDING
- TOWARDS THE END
- PICTURE

Back Cover:
- LIST OF BOOKS BY THE AUTHOR
- PUB. DATE

Middle Panel:
- PICTURE TO GO ALONG WITH
- MIDDLE OF STORY
- MIDDLE OF STORY
- THIS PART OF STORY

Front Cover:
- TITLE WITH COVER ART

Beginning Panel:
- PICTURE OF CHARACTERS
- BEGINNING OF STORY
- LIST OF CHARACTERS
- CHARACTER PICTURE

Motivational Creative Writing

Tips

for Art and the Finished Product

Do not use markers for coloring—the ink tends to be too dark and runny. Large areas colored with markers tend to bleed through the paper.

Use a fine-tip black marker or pen to outline all drawings.

Use a #2 pencil for lettering and art. "Pencil in" everything first and then use the fine point marker to trace over the pencil lines. If you draw with pencil, do not use the pencil for shading. Colored pencils look much better.

Color boldly! Shade heavily! The darker coloring covers up much of the scribbling that can be seen when you color lightly. Use bright, solid colors, and color smoothly.

Watercolor pencils work well for coloring. You can spread and control the color with a damp brush. However, watercolor paints are difficult to work with, and wet paper tends to wrinkle and sag.

Remember: when drawing, the larger the better! Try to fill the pages with your art.

Laminating the cover art adds to the brightness and intensifies the color.

Remember, if you mess up, you can always make another copy and cut and paste it over the mistake!

RUBRICS

- About Rubrics
- Creative Writing Rubric
- Best Rubric Yet!
- Sample Writing Rubric
- Oral Presentation Rubric
- Rubric Form and Scoring Guide

About Rubrics

Teachers should make a rubric (of expectations) for every assignment and review the expectations with students so that they understand the tasks involved and are able to work toward the highest standards set forth. Rubrics have the most meaning when they are developed and agreed upon through a class discussion. Give each writer a copy of the agreed upon rubric of expectations and allow them to use it as a guide for success in the assignment. Generic rubrics fit many assignments and their specific language can be changed to fit each individual teacher, class, and task. Rubrics are tied to instruction, are an important contract between the teacher and the student, and aid in the student's understanding of how the quality of their work is measured.

You might like a 3-place rubric that can turn into a 10-point rubric by adding pluses and minuses and a zero (+ 3 – + 2 – + 1 – 0). The "3 to 10 Rubric" is great when your school's grading system has adopted a percentage scoring criteria for assigning grades. A +3 would transfer to 100%, a 3 would equal 95%, a 3– would be 90% and so on. A 1– is the same as 60%, the lowest percentage offered to those students who at least gave the assignment some attempt. A 0 of course, is 0%, usually reserved for no attempt or missing work.

What follows is a good start for a generic rubric. Modeling a "Mastery" example of a student's assignment is always a great way to communicate what a 3 looks like!

+ 3 = –	**Mastery** (competent, very strong, meets all of the criteria of success, "knocks your socks off" or any other word(s) that would send a clear message of exceptional effort)
+ 2 = –	**Proficient** (working towards Mastery, more strengths than weaknesses, just needs a little more attention, small amount of revision, needs some extra focus, and/or any other term (s) to indicate proficiency)
+ 1 = –	**Emerging** (weaknesses outweigh the strong points, lots of revision, very seldom on target with the assignments criteria, in many cases unclear as to the message of the work, needs major focus and effort)
0 =	(usually given when there is NO effort or for missing work)

This generic rubric can easily be changed and adapted to any creative writing assignment. Simply change the tasks and the expectations.

Creative Writing Rubric

5 THIS WILL KNOCK YOUR SOCKS OFF!
>Project completed and published on time
>All of the formatted steps followed and done well
>Creative and original work
>Ideas clearly communicated
>Author's personality imprinted on the writing task
>Effective and creative word choices and usage
>Sentence fluency and variety
>Correct capitalization, punctuation, and spelling
>Artwork well done, organized, and with extra effort

4 YOU ARE ALMOST THERE, JUST A LITTLE MORE EFFORT!
>Project completed and published on time
>All of the formatted steps followed
>Creative and original work
>Main idea communicated
>Appropriate word choice and usage
>Adequate sentence sense and minimal sentence errors
>Occasional errors in capitalization, punctuation, and spelling
>Art work well done, organized, and with good effort

3 YOU WILL HAVE TO PUT OUT MORE EFFORT THAN THIS!
>Rushed through or finished at the last minute
>Main idea vaguely communicated
>Some of the formatted steps skipped or poorly done
>Occasional inappropriate or incorrect language usage
>Poor sentence structure, some fragments and run-ons
>Inconsistent use of capitalization, punctuation and spelling
>Average effort on artwork and production of final product

2 YOU SHOW A LACK OF UNDERSTANDING!
>Unorganized, partially complete, not on time
>Format not followed, overall effort poor
>Inappropriate or incorrect language usage
>Lack of sentence sense, with fragments and run-ons
>Minimum effort on artwork and production of final product

1 YOU DID NOT DO THE WORK!
>Poor or no effort, not on time or not submitted
>Format steps not followed

Motivational Creative Writing

Best Rubric Yet !

Rubric Focus	Mastery		Proficient	Emerging	
	5 100%	**4** 90%	**3** 80%	**2** 70%	**1** 60%
------------------------------ Standards:					
------------------------------ Standards:					
------------------------------ Standards:					
------------------------------ Standards:					
------------------------------ Standards:					
Totals for 5-place Rubric						Rubric 5
For % score, add the percents and divide by 5						% Grade

Copyright ©2004 by Incentive Publications, Inc., Nashville, TN.

Motivational Creative Writing

Sample Writing Rubric

Rubric Focus	Mastery 5 100%	4 90%	Proficient 3 80%	2 70%	Emerging 1 60%	
Beginning, Middle, End Standards: WS 3.1 WS 3.3	√					
Dialogue Standards: WS 4.0		√				
Story Flow Standards: WS 3.1 WS 5.2	√					
Character Development Standards: WS 4.1			√			
Strong Verbs, Adjectives Standards: WS 3.3 WS 5.0			√			
Totals for 5-place Rubric	10	4	6			Rubric 5 20/25 4
For % score, add the percents and divide by 5	200	90	160			% Grade 450/5 90%

After the class agrees upon the characteristics of a good creative writing product, take a little time to align the characteristics with your school system's standards for writing. (You will have to do this only once.) Number the creative writing traits with the corresponding standard(s). From then on, just cut and paste the five areas the students are to focus on for each assignment. Use the filled-in rubric as a teaching tool, and the students will gradually learn the standards, too. Not only should the standards drive instruction, but following this pattern will demonstrate accountability. For demonstration purposes, this sample rubric focuses on the Writing Curriculum Standards of: WS 3.1, WS 3.3, WS 4.O, WS 4.1, WS 5.0, and WS 5.2, but it can be adapted to any subject or set of standards.

Oral Presentation Rubric

Student Benchmarks

Novice:	Apprentice:	Proficient:
The student rarely makes eye contact with the audience.	The student makes occasional eye contact with the audience.	The student often makes eye contact with the audience.
The student speaks too softly and indistinctly to be heard.	The student speaks in an audible voice.	The student speaks clearly.
The information is not presented in a logical way.	Information may be understood but is not always presented in a logical way.	The information is presented in a logical way.

Motivational Creative Writing

Rubric Form and Scoring Guide

Rubric Form

Teachers and/or students can use this form to create a personalized rubric for any classroom project.

Brief description of task, product, or performance:

_____

_____

Key elements of task, product, or performance:

_____

_____

Criteria for grading key elements:

_____

_____

Scoring Guide

Use the scoring guide to rate a project's level of effectiveness.

Strong: _____

_____

Satisfactory: _____

_____

Needs Improvement: _____

_____

Needs Significant Work: _____

_____

Unacceptable: _____

_____